Praise for *Leading*

"*Leading Academic Change* offers important insights regarding the challenges and opportunities present during this extraordinary moment in the history of higher education. Drawing from her decades of leadership in the academy, Elaine sets forth a compelling case for reexamining traditional educational structures and hierarchies and exploring possibilities for transforming our models, guided by the profound principle that 'nothing is more powerful in higher education than uncompromising commitment to student success.'"—*John J. DeGioia*, *President of Georgetown University*

"One of America's best university presidents has written a brilliant book that will surely inspire and instruct other educational leaders. Each page overflows with eloquence, wisdom, evidence, and powerful examples. This book is perhaps Maimon's most significant gift to higher education. Anyone interested in transformation must read it."—*Shaun R. Harper*, *Clifford and Betty Allen Professor, University of Southern California Rossier School of Education*

"Raising the bar for student success is critical for America as it confronts the challenges of the twenty-first century. This book is an indispensable resource for those committed to improving their institutions in the interest of student success."—*Muriel A. Howard*, *President, American Association of State Colleges and Universities (AASCU)*

"Academic leaders—be they presidents, faculty, staff, or community partners seeking to improve higher education and K–12 schools—will reap tremendous value from *Leading Academic Change*. Maimon has done a masterful job that will galvanize leaders to adopt an equity-minded, student-centered framework to increase student access, engagement, and success."—*Martha J. Kanter*, *Executive Director, College Promise Campaign, former U.S. Under Secretary of Education* (2009–2013)

"This book is a must-read for college teachers and administrators who seek a positive, principled response to the problems besetting U.S. higher education."—*David R. Russell*, *Professor of English, Iowa State University*

LEADING ACADEMIC CHANGE

May 30, 2018

LEADING ACADEMIC CHANGE

Vision, Strategy, Transformation

*For Nevine,
a colleague
who leads
academic
change
in
higher
education.*

Elaine P. Maimon

Foreword by Carol Geary Schneider

*Warm regards,
Elaine*

Sty/us

STERLING, VIRGINIA

Published by Stylus Publishing, LLC.22883 Quicksilver Drive
Sterling, Virginia 20166-2102

Library of Congress Cataloging-in-Publication Data
Names: Maimon, Elaine P., author.
Title: Leading academic change : vision, strategy, transformation/
Elaine P. Maimon ; foreword by Carol Geary Schneider.
Description: Sterling, Virginia : Stylus Publishing, LLC, [2018] |
Includes bibliographical references.
Identifiers: LCCN 2017032806 (print) |
LCCN 2017058367 (ebook) |
ISBN 9781620365694 (Library networkable e-edition) |
ISBN 9781620365700 (Consumer e-edition) |
ISBN 9781620365670 (cloth : alk. paper) |
ISBN 9781620365687 (pbk. : alk. paper)
Subjects: LCSH: Education, Higher--Aims and objectives--United
States. Educational change--United States.
Classification: LCC LA227.4 (ebook) |
LCC LA227.4 .M345 2018 (print) |
DDC 378/.01--dc23
LC record available at https://lccn.loc.gov/2017032806

13-digit ISBN: 978-1-62036-5670 (cloth)
13-digit ISBN: 978-1-62036-5687 (paperback)
13-digit ISBN: 978-1-62036-5694 (library networkable e-edition)
13-digit ISBN: 978-1-62036-5700 (consumer e-edition)

Printed in the United States of America

All first editions printed on acid-free paper
that meets the American National Standards Institute
Z39-48 Standard.

Bulk Purchases

Quantity discounts are available for use in workshops and for
staff development.
Call 1-800-232-0223

First Edition, 2018

10   9   8   7   6   5   4   3   2   1

For all those who lead change in the classroom; in journalism; and in life, especially Mort, Gillian, and Alan

CONTENTS

Meeting the Needs of America's New Majority Learners

In recent decades, higher education has opened its doors wider than ever before, reaching out to embrace students and communities that previously had very limited access or no access at all to higher learning. Today, students of color, working adults, and students from low-income backgrounds constitute a new majority in postsecondary education. Helping these students gain a quality college education holds extraordinary promise—certainly for the students themselves but, more than is often recognized, for our nation as well. Because they already are the new majority in postsecondary study, these students are now, and will remain, the indispensable talent pool on which America's future depends (Merisotis, 2016).

Finding a way to develop new majority students' full potential— as working professionals; civic participants; and thoughtful, resilient, generative people—is arguably this nation's most urgent postsecondary education priority. In *Leading Academic Change: Vision, Strategy, Transformation* Elaine P. Maimon tackles this challenge head-on.

Readers will find in these pages an inspiring and immensely useful guide, not only for policy leaders' student success goal of "closing the completion gaps" but also for the larger goal of creating educationally empowering environments in which new majority students will complete their studies as well as gain the breakthrough advantages of a high-quality liberal—and liberating—college education.

The conception of a purposeful and public-spirited liberal education set forth in these pages applies directly to students' career interests and to all majors, including majors whose titles "sound like a job." Whether students aspire to be accountants, health workers, or the entrepreneurs of tomorrow, Maimon wants all of them to emerge with well-anchored, big-picture knowledge and the judgment to connect knowledge with ethical action. But to help students actually achieve this kind of education, educators themselves will need to break free of old assumptions about how students should proceed through college. *Leading Academic Change* shows us how.

The Maimon Action Plan: If Success is the Goal, Redesign the Way Students Learn

What will it take to help the nation's aspiring new majority students go the distance not only to the credential but also to the expansion of opportunity they both seek and need? And, equally important, how can educators resist the trends already pushing postsecondary education toward a multitiered educational system, in which some college students gain what business leaders call the *power skills* needed for leadership and innovation, while millions of other students are steered to job training programs keyed to available jobs with little or none of the big-picture inquiry learning that liberal education is intended to provide?

Leading Academic Change speaks directly to these questions and more. Maimon herself is a seasoned leader whose entire career has been devoted to supporting new levels of student success in learning, for traditional learners and new majority learners alike. The primer she provides in these pages combines a transformative vision for the future of U.S. higher education with a wealth of practical wisdom gleaned from a lifetime of influential work on the frontlines of educational reform and redesign.

I first met Maimon nearly four decades ago in a time when both of us recognized, from different vantage points, that standard higher education practice was working badly for the "new" students who were already arriving on many college campuses and for a good fraction of "traditional" students as well. Maimon was, at the time, already widely heralded as one of the founding mothers of what is now called the "writing across the curriculum" (WAC) movement. I, like many in my generation, was desperately seeking guidance on how to help career-minded college students with weak academic skills develop the proficiency they clearly needed in writing, evidence-based thinking, and other liberal education fundamentals. We became colleagues, and I have been learning with and from her ever since.

Maimon and her WAC colleagues became tireless champions of testing the potential power of writing as inquiry learning across multiple disciplines from the first to the final year and creating assignments and pedagogical practices that would give students themselves a stake in their own development of voice and inquiry power.

WAC was a breakthrough reform in its own right, inspiring faculty across the country to recast the foundational writing course and add recurring practice in inquiry writing to their majors and writing-intensive senior capstones to their degree requirements. In 2017, my former colleagues at the Association of American Colleges & Universities (AAC&U) reported from a nationwide study of students' course-based assignments at broad-access institutions that students performed better on writing than on the other intellectual skills examined (Rhodes & McConnell, 2017). These researchers credited the writing reforms of recent decades for this encouraging outcome.

Equally important, however, WAC both proclaimed and modeled a critical lesson for *all* the proficiencies students need to develop through college studies. The lesson is this: No powerful capability can be developed within the space of a single course. It's not that first-year writing courses were a bad idea; rather, they were *insufficient* for the task at hand.

WAC taught the academy that students need to practice essential learning outcomes like writing and analytic inquiry again and again, in diverse inquiry contexts and at progressively more challenging levels, to fully develop their intellectual skills and become adept in applying these proficiencies to new settings and challenges. The same principle applies to other cross-cutting capabilities like information literacy, quantitative fluency, or ethical reasoning. Each of these liberal learning capabilities needs frequent practice in multiple learning contexts, including students' majors, before students can reasonably be expected to demonstrate and deploy their proficiency.

WAC also sent another important message to higher education, one Maimon has modeled persistently in her own career and illustrates yet again in these pages. The lesson is this: It will take comprehensive redesign, not just tinkering around the edges of standard educational practice, to help the nation's aspiring new majority learners reap the full benefit of an empowering education. Practices invented a century ago, like a menu of disconnected broad survey–type liberal arts and sciences courses in the first two years (termed *breadth*) and an isolated, stand-alone major (termed *depth*) in the final year, do not work for today's students. In fact, recent research suggests that the chaotic breadth curriculum, sometimes called a cafeteria college model, frequently offered in the first two years of college is itself a factor in the high U.S. dropout rates (Bailey, Jaggars, & Jenkins, 2015). Yet this counterproductive model is still used in many four-year institutions and, indeed, is often imposed by state regulation in public higher education.

I am convinced that education redesign, focused on integrative cross-disciplinary learning and rich in hands-on application, will be the critical next step in building breakthrough success for today's new majority learners. Both to achieve new levels of completion and to prepare graduates for the complex challenges they face at work and in the world, the traditional breadth/depth curriculum invented around 1900 needs a resolutely twenty-first-century do-over. But that do-over needs to keep the hallmark strengths of a liberal and liberating education centrally in view, with new emphasis on both creating connections between liberal learning and career preparation and teaching students to connect knowledge with applied learning and action.

Comprehensive redesign may seem a daunting challenge, to be sure. But the inspiring message of *Leading Academic Change* is that much of the groundwork for the needed redesign has already been done. A core lesson of this book is that educators have all the tools we need—right now—to dramatically accelerate transformative change in the way we educate students, new majority and traditional alike.

High-Impact Practices and More: How to Use the New Evidence on Student Success Practices That Work

If redesign is the goal, what are the resources in hand? As Maimon shows in these chapters, a generation of enterprising educational reformers has already been hard at work testing and developing better ways to educate today's diverse and diversely prepared learners. The good news from their collective efforts is that higher education knows significantly more today than ever before about practices that demonstrably do work, both to increase student persistence in college and to deepen student engagement with learning.

One important resource is the family of faculty-led reform movements collectively termed *high-impact practices* or *HIPs* (Box

F.1). HIPs, as a group, involve students with inquiry learning about complex questions and challenge students themselves to develop evidence-based answers. When done well, HIPs also include collaborative work with diverse peers; faculty; and, often, community-based partners and employers. Finley and McNair's (2013) research shows that the more frequently students participate in HIPs, the more likely they are both to persist in college and to report deeper learning.

Beyond HIPs, there are numerous other innovative practices that have been empirically shown to correlate with increased student persistence and achievement. This family of institution-level student success practices includes mentoring, cultural support groups, intrusive advising, data analytics, reforms in remedial education financial incentives, and taking what Complete College America calls a full "15-to-finish" set of courses each term.

BOX F.1.

HIPs

These practices have been empirically shown to correlate with higher levels of persistence and deeper learning for all students, with what Kuh calls additional compensatory benefit for students from underserved backgrounds. The following list is an amended version of the original set of HIPs identified in Kuh (2008) and, since 2005, central to AAC&U's ongoing inclusive excellence initiative, Liberal Education and America's Promise (LEAP).

- First-Year Seminars and Experiences
- Common Intellectual Experiences
- Learning Communities (thematically linked sets of courses taken in cohorts)
- Writing- and Inquiry-Intensive Courses
- Collaborative Assignments and Projects
- Undergraduate Research
- Diversity/Study Away/Global Learning
- Service-Learning and/or Community-Based Learning
- Internships and Field Experiences
- Capstone Courses and Projects
- ePortfolios

With this wealth of new evidence on student success practices "that work," however, the design challenge becomes ever more urgent. Absent a huge and entirely unlikely infusion of new financial resources, educators can't (and shouldn't, anyway) just add all these practices to augment the traditional undergraduate curriculum. At this juncture, higher education needs new organizing principles—redesign principles—that show educators how to deploy all these resources for maximum benefit to today's diverse students.

From First to Final Year: New Organizing Principles for High Impact Redesign

It is in this search for new organizing principles that Maimon, who has thought and worked systemically for her entire career, helps light the way. *Leading Academic Change* is, among its other strengths, an illuminating user's guide to not only the most promising student success interventions on the horizon but also, and especially, how these practices can be woven together in purpose-driven new designs for students' entire educational experiences.

Maimon currently leads Governors State University (GSU), a highly innovative and starkly challenged broad-access university just south of Chicago, Illinois. As she explains in these pages, GSU recruits students—traditional age and adults alike—who are *first-generation exclamation point*. This term means that many of her students not only are the first in their own families to attend college, but also, and even more challengingly, come to college from neighborhoods where no one they know has ever earned a college degree.

You will need to read the entire book carefully to fully appreciate the redesign sensibility that GSU is modeling. In this foreword, I want to underscore GSU's systemic employment of HIPs to advance the kind of inquiry-led, big-picture, integrative, and applied liberal learning today's career-minded students need. As noted previously, recent research shows that participation in HIPs correlates with both higher persistence and deeper learning, especially for students from underserved backgrounds.

As a result, interest in HIPs has become, as some of us have written elsewhere, a kind of juggernaut across higher education. Especially because of their completion benefits, hundreds of institutions and even some state systems have already made it a goal for students to complete one or two HIPs—perhaps a first-year experience and an internship or other applied learning experience—before they graduate (Kuh, O'Donnell, & Schneider, 2017).

But let's be candid—adding a required HIP or two is still tinkering around the edges of that outdated early 1900s breadth/depth model described previously. It is in this context—in the differences between "tinkering on the margins" and "redesign thinking"—that GSU's reforms provide both educators and students with new design principles for strong learning and increased completion.

Breaking free of that outdated design for a cafeteria curriculum (breadth) in the first two years and specialized but decontextualized learning (depth) in the final two years, Maimon's colleagues have created a spiraling core curriculum that deploys HIPs strategically, from the first to the final year, to ensure that all students participate in inquiry-framed, civic-minded, collaborative, and integrative learning across the entirety of college. Moreover, multiple HIPs are "braided" together in different courses and sequences, thus amplifying their educational power. The whole idea is to erase those long-established dividing lines between so-called broad or general learning and students' career interests and to redeploy cross-disciplinary and integrative liberal learning as an enriching and horizon-expanding context for students' majors and career preparation.

Maimon is the first to say that the model developed at GSU can't and shouldn't just be imported wholesale to another institution. For educational change to take root, each institution must take the time to figure out how to get it right for their particular students and mission. Moreover, it would be wrong to assume that GSU is the only institution that has undertaken this kind of comprehensive redesign (e.g., Peden, Reed, & Wolfe, 2017). The point to be underscored in this foreword is that the organizing principles used at GSU—a first-to-final-year design for inquiry and integrative learning, with HIPs staged strategically across that sequence—hold enormous potential for a higher education enterprise that needs to do dramatically better by today's new majority learners.

Different institutions will translate these redesign principles in different ways. *Leading Academic Change* shows educators everywhere how we can—once and for all—replace the outdated and underperforming breadth/depth curriculum with spiraled and guided pathways, rich in integrative and career-savvy liberal learning, that are purposefully designed to propel new majority learners to new levels of success, both for the learners and the nation dependent on them.

Carol Geary Schneider
Lumina Foundation Fellow
President Emerita, Association of American Colleges &
Universities (AAC&U)

At first I thought of giving this book a one-word title: *Transformation*. But then my editor, David Brightman, did what every good editor should do—he searched for the word on Amazon. He found that prospective readers—prospective searchers, that is—would immediately find books on "weight loss drops" and "concentrated appetite suppression," not on substantive changes in higher education. Accordingly, we transformed the title.

This search research does bring to mind a number of points important to this book. In all fields, *transformation* means big change—change in substance and form. In chemistry, physical change is incremental—mixing together ingredients. Chemical change is substantive and transformational—baking those ingredients into a cake. In theater, through lighting and set design, a scene is transformed from a stable into a castle. In religion, water is transformed into wine.

So this book is about transformation—changing higher education in substance and form, not physical change but chemical change. I argue that this sort of big change is necessary because in the twenty-first century the Internet has radically altered *epistemology*, or human ways of knowing.

Chapter 1, "Transformation in Higher Education," explains this premise and discusses the kind of leadership needed to transform higher education into what the twenty-first century requires. The focus is on presidential leadership, which itself must be transformative rather than transactional. My view of transformational leadership has an identifiable feminist angle, but the cited characteristics, in my experience, are practiced by both women and men.

Chapter 2, "A Vision Without a Strategy Is a Fantasy," unpacks two additional words in the book's title: *vision* and *strategy*. *Vision* is discussed as ways of seeing, and again readers will detect a feminist perspective in my call for both focus and peripheral vision. *Strategy*, a carefully thought-through plan to achieve goals, must be integrally connected to vision. Otherwise, one's sight is clouded by fantasy—pretty pictures that are impossible to achieve.

Chapter 3, "Braiding Together Equity and Quality," discusses my chief motivation for writing the book—the fact that in the United States today, family income is the major determining factor in whether a student will achieve a bachelor's degree. Transforming higher education is essential to preserving our democracy. This chapter makes the argument that bifurcating education into first-job preparation for the poor versus liberal education for the rich undermines our society.

Chapter 4, "Across the Curriculum and Across the Campus: The Infusion Model," discusses writing across the curriculum (WAC), a transformational movement that started in the twentieth century and continues strong in the twenty-first. Proud to be one of the national founders, I tell the story of the grassroots origin of this infusion model and how the concept of infusion is transforming higher education.

Chapter 5, "Exploding the Hierarchical Fallacy: The Significance of Foundation-Level Courses," calls for radical transformation in the significance assigned to foundational, freshman-level courses. I argue that at private liberal arts colleges and regional public institutions, only full-time faculty should teach these courses, and they should do dynamic, multidisciplinary, problem-solving research on how to do the job better. In other words, the best minds on campus should focus on scholarship, curriculum, and pedagogy to accomplish the transformation of first-year students into lifelong learners. Accomplishing these ends calls for disruptive changes in PhD preparation in the humanities, particularly in my own field of English.

Chapter 6, "Rethinking Remediation," calls for research teams including cognitive psychologists, neuroscientists, social workers, and scholars in other fields who have not yet given attention to the concept of underpreparedness to join colleagues in remedial/developmental education in conducting intellectually rigorous and practical inquiry. Until we can apply the fruits of these labors, we must depend on current research and on common sense.

Chapter 7, "Seamless Pathways From the Community Colleges to University Graduation," calls on universities to take more responsibility for creating guided pathways for transfer students. Breaking down hierarchies (chapter 5) will lead to a conversation of equals involving community college and university faculty members and administrators. Together we can help students—many of whom are the first in their families to venture into higher education—to navigate not one but two bureaucracies.

Chapter 8, "A Structured Four-Year Undergraduate Program," draws on research done mainly by the Association of American Colleges & Universities (AAC&U) and Complete College America (CCA) to present a coherent, effective structure for undergraduate education.

Chapter 9, "Putting Students First Is the Best Business Plan," looks at transformational change from a business perspective. Universities are educational institutions first and foremost, but universities are also complex business organizations. The educational mission can be fulfilled only with sound business practices. Putting students first is not only the right thing to do but also good business.

Chapter 10, "Liberal Education and the Search for Truth in a Post-Truth World," brings the book full circle to the idea of liberal education as the key to transformation in universities and in life.

With that broad idea as background, I hope that *Leading Academic Change* will be illuminating not only to people in the academic world but also to broader audiences interested in the twenty-first-century revolution in knowledge, ideas about leadership, and the importance of liberal education to democracy.

This book is both conceptual and deeply personal. I draw many examples from my own academic career and particularly from Governors State University (GSU), where I have served as president for more than a decade. GSU is an example of vision and strategy leading to prize-winning transformations. My colleagues and I would like to convince you that what we have accomplished is eminently scalable. We have moved forward in the worst possible economic circumstances in Illinois. If transformation can happen here, it can happen anywhere.

We believe that vision and strategy can transform any university from an ivory tower to a public square—an *agora*, where, as in Athens, citizens civilly create common ground and share public space for work, governance, and cultural participation. All universities should be public squares. But the regional public universities have a special mission, in the American Association of State Colleges and Universities' (AASCU's) phrasing, to be "stewards of place." Shirley Kenny, former president of Queens College (City University of New York [CUNY]) and Stony Brook (State University of New York), talks about "the romance of public higher education, the possibilities it makes into realities" (personal communication, June 15, 2017).

It is in that spirit that I like to imagine a community garden in the public square. In good times and bad, all participants join in tending the garden. The anthem is Leonard Bernstein's finale to the musical version of Voltaire's *Candide*, a tale of quest, disillusionment, and finally transformation. After unimaginable travails, where everything is emphatically not always for the best in "the best of all possible worlds," Candide and Cunégonde sing poet Richard Wilbur's powerful lyrics, we'll "make our garden grow" (The Leonard Bernstein Office, 2017). If this book had a soundtrack, that would be it. Each of us in leadership positions can transform higher education by transforming our own institutions into public squares with gardens dedicated to the growth and development of our students.

ACKNOWLEDGMENTS

I have always taught students to read pages of acknowledgment and to emulate professional writers by composing these documents. Submitting a paper for a grade is a form of publication—going public with one's work. Formally acknowledging help from others reinforces the concept and practice of peer review and teaches the social nature of writing. Acknowledgment also clarifies its own limits. It's important to point out to students that some unfortunate authors have been sued by individuals who believed that "thank you" was not enough for contributions that should have been duly documented or recognized as coauthorship. Teaching students to avoid plagiarism is clarified when this spectrum of outside influence is mapped out.

Acknowledgment is both necessary and fulfilling. Psychologists have evidence that expressing gratitude is beneficial to a person's health; it's also good for the soul. Reflecting and commenting on contributions of editors, colleagues, friends, and family reinforce membership in a community beyond the computer screen. Writing is less lonely when you amplify voices of those who have engaged with you in conversations about the text.

I am honored to be a member of the community acknowledged here.

Let me begin with Stylus Publishing. David Brightman, senior editor for higher education, illustrates one of the major concepts in this book. He knows how to identify the strengths of a manuscript so that an author is motivated to build on the positive and then make improvements. He and Stylus's president and publisher, John von Knorring, have, over the years, constructed a higher education list that I am proud to be a part of. Their list of authors is rivaled only by their list of restaurants providing the perfect setting for productive discussions. McKenzie Baker is a superb production editor, managing the numerous tasks that transform a manuscript into a book. Kathleen Dyson created a cover design that is a visual expression of the concepts of leadership and transformation. Thanks are also due to all those at Stylus who contributed to the book through their work in marketing, advertising, copyediting, and proofreading. Special thanks to John Gardner for encouraging me to publish with Stylus.

In a sense, I have been working on *Leading Academic Change* for my entire professional life. Professors at the University of Pennsylvania taught me to integrate scholarship and teaching. Special thanks go to Robert Lucid, my brilliant, witty, and much-missed dissertation supervisor; to Malcolm Laws, my mentor in the Penn teaching program; and to Peter Conn, whose approach to preparing graduate students for teaching and scholarship should be widely replicated today (see chapter 5).

My first full-time (non-tenure-track) teaching job was at Haverford College, where I was one of only two women on the faculty. (Another story for another time.) I am grateful that in my early 20s I received from a senior Haverford faculty member one of the best pieces of advice in my professional life: "Always remember, Elaine," he said, "students won't remember very much of what you tell them, but they will remember a great deal of what they tell you." That early version of active learning influenced my academic life and every page of this book.

Thanks to my Beaver College (now Arcadia University) colleagues, who made my years there (1973–1984) a golden time (described in chapters 2 and 4). That Camelot period created an institution committed to writing across the curriculum. Special thanks to my Beaver/Arcadia coauthors of *Writing in the Arts and Sciences* (1981): the late Jerry Belcher, Finbarr O'Connor, Gail Hearn, and Barbara Nodine. Barbara merits a special acknowledgment for particular help on *Leading Academic Change*. My e-mail question about Piaget received an immediate response, even though Barbara was texting from the beach.

Before I joined the Brown University administration as Harriet Sheridan's associate dean of the college, Harriet was a mentor and early creator of writing across the curriculum (see chapter 4). At Queens College (City University of New York), I had the opportunity to work with another lifelong mentor, Shirley Strum Kenny. For six years, at her right hand, I learned what it means to lead academic change from the president's desk.

As the head of the West campus of Arizona State University (ASU West), I began a 21-year partnership that spanned 3 universities (ASU West, University of Alaska Anchorage, and Governors State University [GSU]) with Gebe Ejigu, executive vice president and chief financial officer. The Planning and Budget Advisory Council (PBAC) was his idea (see chapter 9). Thank you, Gebe, for quietly and effectively teaching me so much about the integrity of vision and the strategy necessary to bring about transformation.

This book belongs to the entire community of GSU: students, faculty, staff, administration, and trustees. It's laudable that Illinois public universities are governed by independent boards of trustees. Through the years, the support of the GSU board—particularly of its chairs, Bruce Friefeld, Lorine Samuels, Jack Beaupré, Brian Mitchell, and Pat Ormsby—has encouraged the creativity and nimbleness that have made transformation possible. Special thanks to Ann Vendrely, professor of physical therapy, who chaired the lower-division task force that created GSU's structured four-year undergraduate program (see chapter 8). Deborah Bordelon, provost and vice president for academic affairs, led implementation of the transformation to a four-year, full-service university.

GSU is most fortunate to employ Marco Krcatovich, the world's best director of institutional research and effectiveness. I've checked every GSU fact with Marco, so you can be confident of its accuracy. If any mistake has slipped in, it's my fault, not his.

Penny Perdue, a woman of many talents, deserves her own paragraph. Since 2007, she has been my executive assistant, working behind the scenes to ensure that transformations do not lead to debacles. For this book she has taken on a second role, using vacation time to work as research assistant and copyeditor. In both roles, Penny exhibits excellent judgment, impeccable honesty, and a deep commitment to leading academic change.

Many thanks to the Kresge Foundation and its program officers Caroline Altman Smith, Rebecca Villarreal, and William Moses for recognizing the value and scalability of the Dual Degree Program (DDP) (see chapter 7). Kudos to Linda Uzureau, who transformed herself from GSU's biggest critic to a key leader in creating seamless pathways from community colleges to universities.

The Association of American Colleges & Universities (AAC&U), under Carol Geary Schneider's leadership and continuing under Lynn

Pasquerella, motivates academic change and prepares change agents to develop appropriate strategies. I met Carol in 1981 when she was at the University of Chicago and I was at Beaver/Arcadia. As young educational insurgents, we envisioned transforming universities through core commitments to liberal education. Through the decades, we have worked together and learned from each other. I am proud and grateful that she has written a foreword to this book.

I have been lucky in my university families and also in my personal family. The commitment of my parents to higher education has informed my life. Every day I hear the wisdom and humor of my widowed mother's voice. When we lost her 2 weeks after my high school graduation, my older brother, Stanley, and my sister, Adele, had the unenviable responsibility of filling parental roles for a bereft 17-year-old. Their lifelong encouragement and that of my sister-in-law, Bunny, have provided wings to my academic career and personal life.

My husband, Mort, has supported me on every mile of my journey. He had the vision to resist and transform the gender-stratified cultural expectations of his youth to be a full partner in our shared vision. Teacher, writer, spouse, and father, Mort contributes selflessly to visionary projects, trying hard to endorse my hopeful assumptions. He is also one of the best editors on the planet. Our daughter, Gillian, inspires us every day by infusing liberal education into her elementary school classroom. Our son, Alan, a finalist for the Pulitzer Prize and now an investigative researcher for Centurion (a Princeton-based justice foundation), is a role model for transferring skills from a double major in comparative literature and German studies into work that fulfills his personal mission. He's also a great dad. Our granddaughters, Annabelle and Rosie, personify the future—a time that this book aspires to make better. May the future of higher education and of our nation exemplify Annabelle's kindness and Rosie's exuberance.

I

TRANSFORMATION IN HIGHER EDUCATION

E ducation itself is transformative. From infancy to longevity, formally and informally, education changes lives, materially and spiritually. Classrooms are—or should be—magical spaces. University campuses are definitively places of hope—hope that the status quo is not forever, that low-income students can enter the middle class, that education and research will make the world a better place.

In the twenty-first century, education is going through fundamental transformations. We are experiencing a paradigm shift in learning environments because of an underlying change in epistemology. Never in the history of the planet has information been more readily available. With the click of a key we can find answers to just about any informational question. When the questions are factual, based on common knowledge, we can be relatively confident about the answers.

If we want to know the date of President Abraham Lincoln's assassination, Google will find the answer in seconds—April 15, 1865. At the moment of Lincoln's death, who became the 17th president of the United States? Easy: Andrew Johnson. Was Andrew Johnson impeached? Yes. What does *impeached* mean? Google is still sufficient—he was indicted by the U.S. House of Representatives (that's the impeachment) and, according to procedures spelled out in the Constitution, put on trial by the U.S. Senate "for high crimes and misdemeanors." Was he convicted and removed from office? No. He was tried by the Senate in the spring of 1868 and acquitted by one vote. Thank you, Google. The facts are indisputable and readily available. In the digital age, *information* is at our fingertips.

In contrast, another apparently straightforward question is much trickier. What is the date of William Shakespeare's birth? Wikipedia, to its credit, gives the date of Shakespeare's baptism as April 26, 1564, and then references his birth date as April 23, 1564. Actually, we don't know the exact date of Shakespeare's birth, so celebrations are frequently held on April 23, the date of his death in 1616. Even with seemingly simple information, students must learn to evaluate sources and ask questions.

Knowledge involves the ability to assess and then integrate information into a meaningful whole. Knowledge about the 17th U.S. president, to continue the Andrew Johnson example, would include an understanding of the challenges when he took office on the day of Abraham Lincoln's assassination at the end of a bloody American Civil War. What was Johnson doing to overcome wartime bitterness and hatred and reconcile the North and the South? What were the positions of the Republicans and Democrats on civil rights for the emancipated slaves? What were the reasons for Johnson's impeachment? What motivated the majority of House members to impeach Johnson and the majority of Senate members to acquit him? Knowledge would, in short, involve assessing factual accounts, thinking critically about information, accurately reconstructing a long-ago historical environment, making sound judgments about what happened and what did not, and finally integrating what is known into meaning and understanding.

Wisdom goes even further. Wisdom involves the capacity to apply knowledge effectively to new situations. In terms of the Andrew Johnson example: How do these long-ago circumstances in the United States apply to the aftermath of civil wars in other nations in other times? How do the repercussions of the American Civil War apply to the Truth and Reconciliation Commission in South Africa? How might we define *political courage* in highly partisan situations? Should questions involving slavery, freedom, and human dignity be evaluated within a context of history and culture or within a framework of universality? Wisdom would involve applying concepts from one set of circumstances to very different contexts, defining the underlying issues, considering ethical and moral implications, engaging in problem-solving, and making judgments.

Felten, Gardner, Schroeder, Lambert, and Barefoot (2016) describe the creation of knowledge and its wise applications in the following clear, direct terms: "It [education] is about learning how to learn, asking good questions, analyzing data and information, putting whatever is going on in the world into perspective, and making sound, informed decisions" (p. ix). The Internet is a sea of information. Students must learn to be skilled swimmers in their quest for knowledge and wisdom.

The transformative power of the printing press in the fifteenth century is radically surpassed by the Internet in the twenty-first century. The resulting change in epistemology should be liberating, freeing instructors to focus on evaluating, connecting, and applying information, leading to the discovery of knowledge and the attainment of wisdom. But some educators are still stuck in the dissemination of information. Underlying all other changes discussed in this book is the necessity for this epistemological transformation.

How do we create learning environments that will transform the communication of information into knowledge and wisdom? That is the key challenge for twenty-first-century higher education. This transformation is essential for student success. In civic life and in careers, successful people will be those who are not merely repositories of information but who are makers of knowledge and strivers toward wisdom.

Too often when the topics are transformation, revolution, and disruption, technology is invoked as a panacea, as if sitting students in front of a computer will, on its own lead, them to knowledge and wisdom. Certainly, computers have in a sense caused the revolution in epistemology, but the necessary educational transformations involve people experiencing intellectual change and sharing the personal and societal implications. As Stephen Hawking (2015) says, "Our future is a race between the growing power of technology and the wisdom with which we use it." This book is about human transformations in the digital age.

The history of higher education in the United States, long before the Internet, exemplifies transformation. As Steven Mintz (2017) affirms, "Transformation is as much a part of the history of higher education as continuity." The Morrill Act of 1862 established something that had never existed before—opportunities for nonmembers of the privileged classes to explore the world of ideas, including citizenship in a democracy. Low-income students came from the nation's farmlands to attend new public land-grant universities. In 1944, the GI Bill further expanded opportunities in higher education to World War II veterans from all regions—urban, suburban, and rural. These first-generation college students transformed campuses from Cambridge to Chicago to Los Angeles with new intellectual energy. They countered the prediction of devolution stated bluntly by Robert Maynard Hutchins, president of the University of Chicago (1929–1951), who said, "Colleges and universities will find themselves converted into *hobo jungles*" (as cited in Field, 2008). Instead, U.S. higher education continued its transformation from elitism to what the Association of American Colleges & Universities (AAC&U) calls "inclusive excellence" (AAC&U, n.d.c.).

As the positive results of the GI Bill became evident, the United States moved forward in the 1950s with an even broader commitment to transforming higher education: the major expansion of community colleges, supported by a combination of state and local taxes, to offer opportunities close to students' homes, wherever those homes might be. The GI Bill had already brought students older than the traditional high school graduate to higher education. Community colleges specifically invited adults to explore a second chance for postsecondary study. This enhanced opportunity to go to college countered worldwide practices of early—and usually irreversible—tracking of students into academic and nonacademic pathways.

These historical transformations required new ways of thinking about higher education and democracy, resulting in major organizational changes in colleges and universities. Many of the land-grant universities of the nineteenth century became public university flagships in the twentieth century. Small four-year public universities, some beginning as teachers' colleges, were established in urban, suburban, and rural regions in every state. These regional public universities form the backbone of service to first-generation college students. Today, history meets epistemology. The imperative for inclusive excellence enters the digital age.

Mintz (2017) observes in the following:

> The academy is often viewed as the institution most resistant to change, but we are in the midst of another era of dramatic

transformation. Pedagogy, delivery modes, instructional staffing, and assessments are all being rethought—driven in part by advances in the learning sciences, cost pressures, and a new generation of students with distinct interests and needs.

Transformation is essential in education and therefore must be a key characteristic of viable universities in the twenty-first century.

Higher education transformation relies on transformative presidential leadership. Judy Rosener (1990), in an article titled "Ways Women Lead" in the *Harvard Business Review*, differentiates between what she calls *transactional* leadership and *transformative* leadership. Although Rosener is not suggesting that transformative leadership is something inherent in the X chromosome, she does illuminate differences in the ways that men and women leaders describe themselves, based on life experiences. I believe that both women and men can be transformative leaders, but I find Rosener's distinctions in style to be informative. Transactional leaders, according to Rosener, view job performance "as a series of transactions with subordinates—exchanging rewards for services rendered or punishment for inadequate performance." Transformative leaders are characterized by "getting subordinates to transform their own self-interest into the interest of the group through concern for a broader goal" (pp. 119–125).

These two styles evoke different behavior because transactional leadership is, in essence, about trade—buying and selling—whereas transformative leadership is about shared ownership—buy-in, rather than buying. The two kinds of leadership look very different. Transactional leaders will tend to be more hierarchical, closed, bullying, and power centered, whereas transformative leaders will be more collaborative, open, communicative, and power sharing. Transformative leadership is more focused on relationships, more open to multiple interpretations, more adaptable to new situations, more flexible in adjusting to new environments, readier to multitask, and capable of paying attention both to the goals themselves and to the process for achieving those goals. Transformative leadership has the power to transform colleges and universities into twenty-first-century institutions.

Based on the following principles, this book explores twenty-first-century transformative leadership and its power to bring about academic change through vision and strategy:

- *Higher education must go beyond the dissemination of information to evaluation, connection, and application.* Twenty-first-century epistemology requires assessing the validity of information, creating knowledge through connecting disparate facts, and developing wisdom by applying knowledge to a wide variety of situations. Curricula, syllabi, and classroom practices should demonstrate this transformation.

- *Low-income, first-generation students deserve high-quality bachelor's degrees with a strong foundation in critical thinking and communication.* In the twenty-first century, preparation for a first job is not enough. Some politicians enjoy saying that the United States needs welders, not philosophers. But experienced welders are already telling us that robotics is taking over manual labor, and successful welders must be project managers who exercise critical thinking and problem-solving to achieve that success. Students who major in philosophy are those who do the best on the Law School Admissions Test (LSAT) because they apply critical thinking to legal situations. As Stephen H. Weiss, former managing director of Neuberger Berman, Inc., said in an interview with AAC&U, "We need more big-picture thinking in the professions and more real-world experience in the liberal arts" (personal communication with Debra Humphreys, vice president of strategic engagement, Lumina Foundation and formerly AAC&U vice president, n.d.). We need lifelong learners, whatever their family income or academic major.

- *Foundation-level courses, like freshman composition, are worthy of the intellectual energies of first-rate, full-time faculty members.* This transformation will require major changes in PhD preparation, especially in English and other humanities disciplines. We need the nation's best scholars to take on the pedagogical and research challenges of foundational education in critical thinking and communication.

- *Universities can provide both a challenging four-year program and high-quality, guided pathways from the community college to university graduation.* Universities should develop logical pathways and special agendas for each of the four years of undergraduate study—foundational courses, exploration of majors, focused study with career implications, and the transfer of learning to broader contexts. At the same time, universities must create pathways for transfer students, especially those from community colleges. The coherence of education across more than one institution cannot be left exclusively to the community college or to the students themselves. Universities have obligations to connect with community colleges to encourage a coherent program of study there, providing incentives for the completion of the associate degree before moving on to the university's junior year.

- *Twenty-first-century higher education requires high-impact practices, like writing across the curriculum (WAC).* Educational practices, including writing in all courses, student–faculty research partnerships, long-term projects, community service, civic engagement, and study abroad, move classrooms away from the simple dissemination of information to the creation and application of knowledge.

- *Mentoring is essential to student success.* The 2014 Gallup-Purdue Index Report, *Great Jobs, Great Lives,* studied more than 30,000 college graduates across the United States. The study found that great lives after graduation did not depend on the type of college or university students attended—public or private, large or small. But

  if graduates had a professor who cared about them as a person, made them excited about learning, and encouraged them to pursue their dreams, their odds of being engaged at work more than doubled, as did their odds of thriving in their well-being. (p. 6)

- *We must substitute a strength model for a deficit model.* The work of Shaun Harper and his colleagues (University of Pennsylvania's Center for the Study of Race and Equity in Education and the Race & Equity Center at the University of Southern California) explains the necessity of recognizing and validating students' strengths, connecting the knowledge they have with new ideas and applications. Identifying strengths is hard work, requiring breaking through barriers and inculcating confidence and trust. The widely used deficit model, however, is the easy way out, emphasizing the correction of surface features rather than in-depth understanding.

- *Strategic planning and budget reallocation depend on transparency and inclusiveness—and can be done in a unionized environment.* This book rejects the argument that "we can't do this because. . . ." Yes, budget reallocation—a huge challenge in higher education—is almost certainly required. But transformation is essential, whatever the overall fiscal situation.
- *Higher education is a public good and merits generous investments at the state and federal level.* Regarding higher education as merely a private good—a commodity—is remarkably short sighted. Twenty-first-century transformations will lead to improvement in the economy, community spirit, social justice, and the quality of life for all.
- *Student enrollment in universities is not a zero-sum game.* Democracy depends on our attracting and serving students who are not currently matriculating in rigorous four-year programs or not completing them. Public regional universities like Governors State University (GSU) and others such as American Association of State Colleges and Universities (AASCU) universities are playing a highly significant role in educating these first-generation students. Private universities, especially those smaller and less famous than the short list of the highly selective and heavily endowed, have an unfulfilled mission to serve new student populations, including community college transfers and returning adults.
- *Students can gain an outstanding university education without being saddled with crushing debt.* Federal and state support is important. But universities must also help students and their families develop financial literacy, treating a modest amount of borrowing as an investment but keeping long-term debt as low as possible.
- *Nothing is more powerful in higher education than uncompromising commitment to student success.* If we keep this principle in the forefront, all transformations are possible.

In the following chapters, I will draw examples from my experiences over four decades at the following educational institutions: Haverford College, Arcadia University (née Beaver College), University of Pennsylvania, Queens College (City University of New York [CUNY]), Arizona State University West (ASU West), University of

Alaska Anchorage (UAA), and GSU. After starting out as an English professor, I have now spent more than 20 years, under various titles, as campus chief executive officer. In each instance and in different circumstances, I have had opportunities to lead academic change. GSU in suburban Chicago has yielded—and continues to yield—remarkable opportunities to create a model twenty-first-century university. I will therefore draw substantially on this living context for transformational change in U.S. higher education.

2

A VISION WITHOUT A
STRATEGY IS A FANTASY

When universities search for presidents, *vision* usually tops the list of presidential sought-after characteristics. But what does *vision* actually mean? It does not mean fanciful musings. *Vision* literally means sight—the ability to see clearly, to notice what goes unnoticed. Often the emphasis is on seeing into the future, but that ability is dependent on a credible perception of the past and a vivid observation of the present. Vision certainly requires focus—undeterred attention to mission and goals. But—and this point is often missed—it also requires peripheral vision.

In other words, twenty-first-century university leaders must have double vision: focus and peripheral. Anthropologist Mary Catherine Bateson (1994), in her book *Peripheral Visions: Learning Along the Way,* describes the

> multiple levels of focus [that are] common style for women who have spent years with one ear open for the cry of an awakened child, the knock of someone making a delivery, the smell of burning that warns that a soup left to simmer slowly has somehow boiled dry. (p. 96)

Bateson argues that women are particularly prepared for double vision because of life experiences. I would say that greater diversity in academic leadership highlights the importance of this quality for both women and men.

Although university leaders must focus on goals—balancing the university's budget, increasing enrollment, raising millions for the capital campaign—some of the most significant issues may be emerging from the periphery—the offended tone in the voice of the academic senate president, the student leader's hint of mobilizing discontent, the special gleam in the eye of a potential donor when the subject of learning communities is mentioned. Women's life experiences may offer special preparation in keeping eyes on the prize, while simultaneously observing the processes involved in winning the prize, but this double vision is necessary to all twenty-first-century academic leaders.

Peripheral vision also helps leaders to see multiple meanings, rather than being satisfied with what Bateson calls "the rhetoric of merely," reducing interpretation to simplistic explanations like, "That dean is merely looking for a bigger budget," or "That student is merely a C student," or "That donor is too conservative to consider scholarships for needy students." As Bateson (1994) says, "Many tales have more than one meaning. It is important not to reduce understanding to some narrow focus, sacrificing multiplicity" (p. 11).

Peripheral vision involves an ability to understand the persuasive powers of both words and actions, what I call the *rhetoric of words* and the *rhetoric of actions*. An example: A male president was lamenting to his vice presidents (six male, one female) that the university as a whole did not seem convinced by his stated commitment to women's leadership. He, in fact, charged the vice president for public relations (a male) to work out a communication strategy to clarify that point. The president was sharply focused on the rhetoric of words. He missed seeing—and this matter was hardly on the periphery—that he had made embarrassingly few female senior appointments. On the periphery, completely unseen by the president, was his tendency on social occasions to talk almost exclusively to the immediate male subordinate of the one female vice president, embarrassing her in public settings and sending messages about his comfort level, or lack thereof, with female peers.

Peripheral vision also means the ability to see the difference between *speed* and *haste*. Twenty-first-century leadership requires responses in real time—in other words, *speed*. But *haste*, as in "act in haste, repent at leisure," can actually slow things down because of the time and effort necessary to repair the damage of acting without appropriate information or necessary processes. Focus, without peripheral vision, can lead to strategies best described as "ready, fire, aim." Speed requires the peripheral vision that produces readiness

for opportunity. A university president may find out about the possibility for a multimillion-dollar grant only two weeks before the
application deadline, but a president with peripheral vision has
understood months in advance that an opportunity in the general
area of the request for proposal was possible and has prepared the
appropriate university officers to be ready, or she has had the fore-
sight to hire people who are able to create that readiness. "Ripeness
is all," writes Shakespeare (1606, 5.2.15) in *King Lear*. Peripheral
vision leads to ripeness—to readiness. We have often heard people
complain that they never have good luck, yet we have personally seen
them get lucky, although they never noticed. Peripheral vision helps
us be ready for luck.

Another feature of peripheral vision is respect for people's time.
Some presidents believe that their vice presidents must be available
24/7. Meetings are called on short notice—or no notice. No one
has an agenda, and the meetings rarely start or end on time. Assignments are made to multiple cabinet members without any structure
for cooperation, so people waste time and spin wheels. Full, focused
commitment to a job is better achieved when there is some predict-
ability about time commitments, allowing for arrangements to be
made for family responsibilities. If a president acts as if 100% of vice
presidents' time is his due, then his team will actually be less effective, burned out, and apprehensive about making any commitment
of personal time. In contrast, if a president is generally respectful of
people's time, then, when a true crisis emerges that requires round-
the-clock activity, the vice presidents will be more willing and able
to meet those demands.

Peripheral vision allows a team of vice presidents and close
advisers to feel comfortable presenting a diversity of viewpoints,
rather than rubber-stamping the president's initial idea. Focus on
that one good idea may prevent the president from seeing the inherent problems or the advantages of another approach. I have actually
been in the room when a president went around the table of his
chief advisers with the following request: "Tell me why this is a good
idea." This president was putting on blinders, blocking peripheral
vision. Discomfort with opposing points of view leads to "yes men,"
cronyism, and unhealthy organizations.

Clearly vision, both focused and peripheral, is necessary to presidential success. But vision without strategy will lead nowhere. A

strategy is more than a plan. In fact, strategic thinking, like vision, involves sight and insight—seeing many pathways through a complexity of choices and discovering the best route to success. Strategic planning requires broad-based ownership from the campus community. Presidential leadership depends on listening carefully to many ways to achieve university goals and then helping stakeholders articulate and map out the path forward.

As chief executive officer at three universities—ASU West, UAA, and GSU—I have led many strategic planning processes, but I must confess that I learned most of these presidential skills very early in my career when I was a writing program administrator.

In the spring of 1975, I was in my second year as a part-time English instructor at what was then called Beaver College (now Arcadia University), located in suburban Philadelphia. I was also a wife and the mother of a five-year-old and a two-year-old. I was busy adapting to change. My new assignment, in addition to caring for a toddler and a kindergartner, was to direct the writing program at Beaver, although my PhD preparation was in literature. My status at the college could not have been more marginal. Although I had been assigned a full-time, tenure-track position for the following fall, I was the most junior of junior faculty members. Furthermore, in those days, no one really knew much about directing writing programs.

Many women presidents have followed unusual career paths and developed special skills and perspectives through jobs on the periphery of institutions. From reading hundreds of CVs over the years, I know that men are much more likely to follow a linear, focused career path to the presidency: from assistant to associate to full professor, to department chair, dean, provost, and then president. The role of composition director is definitely on the periphery, although less so now than in 1975, thank goodness.

As composition director, I developed a passion for teaching students to write that has informed my entire professional life. I saw very early that writing and learning were intertwined in complex ways. Consequently, a composition director could go only so far without full campus cooperation. Before WAC became a movement or even had a name, it was clear to me as a young, marginalized assistant professor that it takes a campus to teach a writer. My career as a university administrator is rooted in that early passion. I learned to do curriculum design, faculty development, strategic planning, budgeting, and fund-raising because I needed all those skills to rally the campus to use writing as a tool for learning and to see student writing as the signature of the institution.

WAC is a movement that continues to inform curriculum and pedagogy in the twenty-first century. WAC, outliving the century in which it was named, is the acknowledged seedbed of learner-centered education and other significant educational movements. WAC is the original high-impact practice. As one of the national founders, I gained valuable early experience in developing a double vision: focus and peripheral. My focus was on a project that by definition had to involve the entire institution. Yet, from the periphery, without any formal institutional power, I had to develop a strategic plan for the project. As a writing program administrator, I learned that a vision without a strategy is a fantasy, and I developed the following skills and attitudes that have made me a better and more effective president:

- *Listening.* As a young, untenured composition director, I had no choice but to seek advice from colleagues about how to make the writing program more responsive to their students' needs. Thus, I learned a key rule of successful administration: Asking for advice is a better strategy than making suggestions. Listening leads to authentic dialogue and shared ownership of ideas. In other words, I was practicing the concept of *transformational leadership* 15 years before Judy Rosener (1990) coined the term.
- *Intellectual mobility.* As a proponent of WAC, I had to move across bounded areas of the university. A successful twenty-first-century president must also move gracefully across disciplines and inspire faculty members to see the connections among areas of inquiry. One of the biggest challenges today is to encourage faculty members to emerge from disciplinary silos and, while maintaining a sharp focus on particular research interests, to see connections. Multimillion-dollar institutes and centers are established to create intellectual mobility. I learned it young. I could not stay in my office

or library carrel. I had to talk with colleagues in their own buildings across campus, in their laboratories, and on field trips. (Ah, yes, the field trips. It was worth tipping over in the Mullica River as I accompanied the biology club on a field trip to explore the New Jersey Pine Barrens.) I had to travel across the Pine Barrens and across the curriculum to learn the differing perspectives of biologists, historians, and literary critics. I had to see through their eyes what looked different from various vantage points and what values were held in common.

- *Putting students' interests first.* Spending time carefully reading what students write is a powerful reminder that colleges and universities must address the aspirations of students. No matter how full of catchphrases and mistakes, students' early attempts at sophisticated discourse provide a visible map of challenges to our pedagogic and research capacities. Student writers are individuals, not numbers on a registrar's list. It is important to discover students' strengths, rather than perpetually focus on their deficits. Today, whatever the administrative issue—budget, scheduling, scholarships, differential pricing for different majors—I believe that the best guide to making the right decision is to consider the best interests of students.

With these principles to guide me, I moved into increasingly responsible professorial and administrative positions. When I left Arcadia University, I was a full professor and associate vice president, ready to assume the responsibilities of my next position, associate dean of the College at Brown University. After 18 years in private, selective higher education, I then exercised the flexibility that I had learned on the periphery to become a dean at Queens College, CUNY. My next move was to the position of chief campus officer (with the unlikely title of provost) at ASU West. I then served as the chancellor of UAA. And I am now the president of GSU in the south suburbs of Chicago.

As I reflect on my career, it is clear that my early experiences on the periphery gave me a crash course in developing focus, peripheral vision, and strategic thinking. Many women presidents have similar stories—not in the details but in the special learning opportunities inherent in their life experiences. Some might still insist that the best pathway to the presidency is a steady forward march through the academic ranks, without time devoted to marginal enterprises like directing writing programs. I would argue that those who take a few detours, thereby strengthening their peripheral vision, may be acquiring better preparation for twenty-first-century leadership than those who follow more conventional paths. I would urge search firms and boards of trustees to take this point into account when they review CVs that look somewhat unconventional.

In 2007, when I became president of GSU, the institution seemed perfectly situated for developing strategies to fulfill its original vision as an experimenting university. GSU was founded in 1969 by a group of Chicagoland visionaries, who imagined a public university close enough to the city for easy commuting, yet far enough away to offer a bucolic setting—a tranquil option for urban, suburban, and rural students. GSU is definitely a campus where the prairie meets the city.

The original GSU experiments understandably reflected innovations in vogue during the time. One experiment was to make this new public campus an upper-division university, specializing in transfer students and returning adults. The vision was clear, but the strategy was questionable for GSU and for other "senior universities" founded in the 1960s, 1970s, and 1980s. On the surface, it looks reasonable to encourage students to begin at community colleges and then to complete their bachelor's degrees at universities specifically focused on transfer students and returning adults. The problem is that it doesn't work, academically, psychologically, or financially.

During the decades of upper-division university presence— only one or two still remain—the dismal statistics did not change. According to the National Student Clearinghouse Research Center (2016a), no more than 16% of high school graduates who began at a community college and aspired to a bachelor's degree completed the degree within 6 years. This mismatch between vision and actuality resulted from strategic flaws. Many students seeking the economic advantages of beginning higher education in the community college are first-generation college students. Yet, with the community college/transfer approach, we ask them to navigate not one but two complex bureaucracies.

Even with the best institutional cooperation, including clear articulation agreements, the students themselves require personal guidance. Because most first-generation college students work while they go to school, they may erroneously assume that part-time attendance is their only option, stretching out their studies over several years, losing the coherence of more concentrated academic work, and actually paying more in the long run by losing out on federal and state grants—money that does not have to be paid back. It is only recently that Complete College America (CCA) has done convincing research on the academic desirability of "15 to Finish." Taking 15 credits per semester is a full-time load, but most students, with guidance on time management, can successfully complete this course work while also holding a job. But in the heyday of the senior university, the overwhelming majority of students were part-time, taking only one or two courses per semester and stretching out their studies over too many years.

Psychologically, the senior university did not have a recognizable place in the mental framework of most students, families, and high school guidance counselors. When people heard *2-year*, they assumed GSU was a community college. Even when GSU developed the Dual Degree Program (DDP), an award-winning partnership with Chicagoland community colleges, high schools did not permit the university to recruit for this outstanding guided pathway (see chapter 7 for more on the DDP). As a result, enrollments at upper-division universities rarely exceeded 2,000 full-time equivalent (FTE) students. At GSU, with the greatest possible efforts, undergraduate enrollments increased slightly from 1,475 FTE in 2003 to 1,958 FTE in 2012, but never reached 2,000 FTE. After 2 years with a 4-year undergraduate program, GSU's undergraduate FTE enrollment in 2016 was 2,247. From 2003 to 2016, the overall FTE enrollment, combined undergraduate and graduate, increased from 2,852 to 3,888. This across-the-board increase is clearly the result of becoming a full-service, comprehensive university.

Founded in 1984, the ASU West campus, where I served as chief campus officer (1996–2004), had static enrollment until 2002, when it transformed into a four-year institution. To make the static enrollment even more problematic, ASU West offered an innovative, brilliant, interdisciplinary curriculum in the arts and humanities, but its population of transfer students, most of whom had strictly instrumental goals, signed up predominantly for professional course work in business, education, and human services. Until ASU West offered a four-year undergraduate program, talented interdisciplinary faculty members had too few students to teach. The upper-division experiment ignored an important fact: first- and second-year students taking foundational, liberal education courses are necessary to support majors in the arts, humanities, and social sciences.

From a financial standpoint, the upper-division university is difficult to sustain. How is it possible, for example, to make sure that liberal arts faculty members in English, history, and philosophy have a full load of courses when the majors are small and they have no opportunity to teach lower-division introductory courses? Both ASU West and GSU faced these problems. Each university also has a beautiful multiacre campus, which is difficult to justify without robust and growing enrollment. As upper-division universities, both ASU West and GSU scheduled most classes at night, with the splendor of the campus cloaked in darkness. Furthermore, this arrangement ignores the needs of an important adult population—the parents of school-age children. It also assumes that working adults are rigid in their expectations of course scheduling.

Ironically, GSU's founding visionaries worked with philanthropists and state officials to set aside 753 acres, with lakes, woodland, and an internationally acclaimed sculpture park. Yet, in the upper-division era, most students were part-time and experiencing this loveliness only at night. A vision, including night vision, without a strategy is a fantasy.

Increasing enrollment means more students paying tuition, more money in the income fund, and the ability for GSU to continue charging the lowest tuition and mandatory fees in Chicagoland. Instituting lower division at GSU has enabled the university to keep our tuition affordable and to fulfill the original special mission to underserved students.

In that sense, *transformation*, rather than *reinvention*, is the better term to apply to GSU. *Reinvention* denotes remaking or redoing something completely—starting over. Transformation is organic.

Today, at GSU we say that innovation is in our DNA, and we mean it. The changes we have implemented in the twenty-first century have their roots in the twentieth century. GSU in the 1970s literally implemented classrooms without walls. The noise level itself made that experiment a failure and led to some strangely configured spaces when the walls went up in the 1980s. Yet, the idea of openness and movement—transparency, intellectual mobility, and flexibility—continues to infuse the GSU spirit. And today the worldwide classroom without walls is the Internet.

The GSU innovators of the last century seriously questioned the effectiveness of course grades in guiding students' development or in evaluating their achievement. Those questions continue to be important today. In the 1970s, for a while, the university functioned without grades. Instead, faculty members would write in-depth evaluations of students' progress. Founding faculty members still joke about ceiling-high portfolios. Aha, portfolios! Once again, GSU was ahead of its time and ahead of the available technology. Although today GSU students receive grades, we have instituted ePortfolios, outcomes assessment, and applications of the Degree Qualifications Profile (DQP) (AAC&U, n.d.a).

In 2007, when I assumed the GSU presidency, the campus community was aware that I had presided over the transformation of the ASU West campus from upper-division to four-year. They asked if that was my goal for GSU. My answer was that our first priority was to find ways to make community college partnerships really work—and then we would see. As we launched our strategic planning process that year, it was clear to all constituencies that the university's highest priority was to increase enrollment. From every perspective—academic, fiscal, and legislative—GSU had to better fulfill its mission by expanding its student base.

We had to begin by being true to our roots. Accordingly, our priority was to develop a plan for seamless student transfer from community colleges. By 2011, we had established the DDP, our scalable approach to guiding community college students through two bureaucracies (more about that in chapter 7). But we were still not sufficiently offering, as our mission statement says, an exceptional and accessible first-class public education to residents of our surrounding communities and to all those traditionally underserved by higher education (www.govst.edu/vision2020). It was essential for GSU to become a full-service public university with a structured four-year undergraduate curriculum, while continuing to provide special access to transfer students and working adults.

At both ASU West and GSU, I had been warned early on that the community colleges would do everything in their power to stop each university from admitting freshmen. In fact, in 1996 at ASU West, I was told by a Maricopa Community College Board member that ASU West would not admit freshmen in my lifetime. I'm happy to say that I was alive and well in 2001 when the first freshmen matriculated at the ASU West campus. Community college leaders understandably, at first, saw university lower-division courses as competition. Yet, it was clear to me in both Arizona and Illinois that the student population interested in a four-year university program does not overlap to a competitive extent with those deciding to begin higher education at the community college. In Arizona, I would look out my office window each morning and watch busloads of freshmen and sophomores shuttling 30 miles in heavy traffic from the ASU West campus in northwest Phoenix to ASU's main campus in Tempe. Moving beyond anecdotal observation, we surveyed these students and obtained quantitative proof that a four-year program on the ASU West campus would not directly compete with neighboring Glendale Community College or other area community colleges.

But proof was not enough, in Arizona or later in Illinois. Trust was the essential element. The community college leaders in both states had to be convinced that freshmean recruitment to the university would not mean the end of strong community college partnerships. In Arizona, before seeking approval from the Board of Regents to admit freshmen, ASU West developed the University/College Center. This program established a site for Glendale Community College—at no cost to the community college—on the ASU West campus. Glendale students in the University/College Center received no-cost ASU identification cards, with full ASU library and other privileges. ASU West student clubs, as well as Glendale Community College clubs, were open to University/College Center students. Glendale Community College faculty members teaching University/College Center students on the ASU West campus were assigned office space and were eligible to trade places in upper-division courses with ASU West faculty members who would teach lower-division University/College Center courses. It was win-win all around.

The trust established by the University/College Center resulted in broad-based community college support when ASU West moved forward to add lower division. As a result, the Board of Regents did not face community college opposition to transforming ASU West into a four-year campus. It also helped that at both ASU West and GSU, we limited freshman enrollment to under 300 full-time students and developed a cohort/learning community model of instruction. At both universities, the existence of strong community college partnerships means that students who do not meet the university's qualifications for admission can be directed to the community college cooperative program. Instead of hearing "no," they can be told, "not yet."

Trust and ownership were essential factors in the transformation of GSU to a full-service university. In the spring of 2011, the campus community began discussions leading to approval of lower division in the three senates: faculty, student, and civil service. At their August 2011 retreat, the Board of Trustees had a thorough discussion of a white paper presenting the concept and overall plan for lower division in the context of the university's strategic plan, Strategy 2015, which had been approved by the board in 2009. Strategy 2015 was not explicit about lower division, but it was clear to the trustees that the goals outlined in that document could not be achieved without this transformation. At their October 2011 meeting, the board voted formal approval of the plan, which we took to the Illinois Board of Higher Education (IBHE) two months later. IBHE was the state body with the power to approve the change. Legislative action was not needed.

We had established trust with our local community colleges through the DDP. With our closest partners we had built shared ownership. We promised that we would do student-centered recruiting, presenting two pathways to a bachelor's degree—either a four-year program at GSU or a clear 2+2 pathway through the DDP. We were able to include in our proposal eloquent letters from community college presidents and private university presidents. Following is an excerpt from a letter written on October 12, 2011, by Eric Radtke, who was then president of our closest community college neighbor, Prairie State College:

The national goal to increase the number of college educated citizens and restore the United States' standing as "first in the world" is one we all agree on. If we are to succeed in reaching that goal, it will take all of our community colleges and universities reaching out to more students to enroll and complete their college degrees. This is particularly true in the low-income, heavily minority region that both Governors State and Prairie State serve, where our college completion rate is significantly lower than in other parts of Illinois and the nation.

Even with this level of community college support and the advocacy of proponents from various internal and external constituencies, the IBHE meeting in December 2011 was lively to say the least. Some readers may wonder about the fast pace for a change of this magnitude. I would argue that the timetable is an example of speed, not haste. GSU carefully planned its proposal for lower division. We then met informally with the IBHE chair to convince her to help us avoid unnecessary delays. As I prepared for the eventful December meeting, my biggest fear was a move to table the proposal. Armed with strong support from all constituencies, I appealed to IBHE to vote our proposal up or down but not to table it. Moving forward with deliberate speed won out. When the sun set on that winter day, GSU had the authority to proceed with planning a lower-division program to be implemented in August 2014.

We immediately worked with the GSU faculty senate to form a lower-division task force, chaired by Ann Vendrely, a highly respected full professor of physical therapy. Vendrely knew that students in professional programs, even in the doctoral-level courses that she taught, needed a strong foundation in writing, critical thinking, and communication. Vendrely's leadership personified the integration of liberal and professional education and went a long way toward motivating faculty colleagues from across the campus to trust the planning process.

Vendrely was (and still is) an active researcher, and she brought a research orientation to the planning process. The white paper presented a framework—270 freshmen (plus or minus 30), a core curriculum based on general education courses required by the Illinois Articulation Initiative (a state law designed to ensure the transferability of courses), small classes (no more than 18 in freshman composition; no more than 30 in any freshman course), and a cohort/learning communities model with every freshman taking at least 3 courses with the same group of students. But there was much to plan within that structure. Vendrely led the task force in surveying research on the freshman experience. They looked particularly at the work of AAC&U, CCA, and the John N. Gardner Institute for Excellence in Undergraduate Education.

My career-long adage is that curriculum change depends on scholarly exchange among faculty members. It worked decades ago with WAC, and it worked with establishing lower division and, more than that, developing a structured four-year undergraduate program. In the intervening years, however, I had learned that the scholarly exchange should be inclusive of all campus employees because everyone at a university from professor to maintenance worker is involved in promoting student learning (Magolda, 2016).

Motivated by the research of the lower-division task force, we developed a plan for symposia for all employees. The first, in March 2012, led by Carol Geary Schneider, then president of AAC&U, was titled Innovation and Creativity in General Education. The second, in October 2012, led by John Gardner and Betsy Barefoot, was titled The Essentials of First-Year Success: Planning for 2014. These symposia established the liberal education base of our planning and the focus on a strong foundation for undergraduate student success. We have continued these campus-wide symposia each semester, with outstanding leaders in WAC, innovative thinking, ePortfolios, and equity. As we completed Strategy 2015 and moved into planning for Vision 2020, the symposium framework encouraged inclusivity. In addition, we sent campus teams to AAC&U workshops on high-impact practices and to conferences on the first-year experience. Our curriculum and pedagogic planning were entirely research based and data driven.

In April 2013, a team from the Higher Learning Commission of the Northwestern States visited GSU to review our substantive change request to add a lower-division program. The following is what they wrote in the report:

> The types of preparation made for this very significant change are being made in tandem with other significant changes in general education programming, assessment processes, institutional research, faculty development and other key areas. Such deep and significant change with such a high level of quality control and in such a short timeframe is rare in higher education.

We were gratified to have this outside validation of our vision and strategy—and of changing our institutional rhythm with speed, not haste.

Simultaneous with developing strategies for a four-year structured undergraduate curriculum, we began in 2011 to plan for GSU's first student residence, Prairie Place. Our vision was to offer a living-learning option involving full-time faculty members living in the residence and creating opportunities for those midnight conversations about the meaning of life that alumni talk about as highlights of their college experience. We also envisioned Prairie Place as a focal point for student life, enhancing experiences for commuters as well as residents by creating a 24/7 campus. We immediately implemented a financial strategy based on selling bonds to support the construction. We also incorporated a classroom into the new building and assigned the resident faculty members to teach freshman seminars. By the third year of operation, Prairie Place was at capacity, demonstrating the successful, strategic implementation of our vision. As we move forward with Vision 2020, we are planning carefully for the right time to start work on Prairie Place II.

Fulfilling our vision overall is the result of formal strategic planning (Strategy 2015 and Vision 2020), but consensus on those documents alone would never have been enough. Successful strategic planning depends on strategic budget investment—putting our money where our mouth is. In chapter 9, I describe the Planning and Budget Advisory Council (PBAC) process, which yielded budget reallocation, the establishment of reserve funds, and the ability to avoid paralysis when Illinois let us down.

The strategies needed to fulfill our vision also depend enormously on communication—internal and external. Decades ago, when I first became an academic administrator, overseeing a grant from the National Endowment for the Humanities (NEH) on WAC, Beaver College's executive vice president gave me the following advice, which I have never forgotten: "Remember, Elaine," he said, "no one reads anything. And the corollary to that is that no one listens to anything. So if you really want to accomplish something, you must develop a communication strategy." And, as I learned through the years, that strategy depends on building trust and on redundancy. The written and spoken words are not enough. Understanding the overall situation, establishing empathy, and creating shared ownership are necessary for the strategic path from vision to fulfillment.

Today, GSU offers undergraduates a structured 4-year program, providing a strong foundation for all students in liberal education. Only full-time faculty members teach freshmen in small classes and conduct research on what some refer to as our highest calling—building on students' strengths to assist in personal transformations, while developing a sense of civic engagement important to our democracy. We continue to fortify our nationally recognized community college transfer program into smooth pathways from 17 partner community colleges, and we have strengthened our commitment as a Completion University, 1 of 5 in a consortium established by the Lumina Foundation for working adults from across the nation to complete bachelor's degrees. We are strategic about the use of high tech and high touch to fulfill our goals. In subsequent chapters, I describe this vision in more detail and outline strategies for transforming visions into realities.

3

BRAIDING TOGETHER
EQUITY AND QUALITY

According to the National Center for Education Statistics, the lowest-achieving, highest-income students are more likely to complete a university degree than the highest-achieving, lowest-income students (as cited in Gould, 2012). In a democracy, family income should not be the deciding factor on whether or not a student achieves a university degree.

What do we know about what helps college students be successful? Let's look at the results of a recent, large-scale Gallup (2015) poll, affirming decades of academic research. The vast majority of college students believe that an investment in college is worthwhile if they have had the following "Big Six" experiences. And we know that low-income and first-generation students benefit from these experiences even more.

1. A professor who made them excited about learning
2. Professors who cared about them as individuals
3. A mentor who encouraged them to pursue their goals and dreams
4. The experience of working on a long-term project
5. An internship where they applied what they were learning
6. Involvement in extracurricular activities

Please note the overlap of these experiences with AAC&U's high-impact practices (Kuh et al., 2008; Kuh & O'Donnell, 2013).

What does it take to braid equity and quality together? My answer: It takes vision, strategy, action, and leadership. This question and its response informed GSU's transformation, acknowledged in March 2015 by the American Council on Education/Fidelity Investments Award for Institutional Transformation.

GSU energetically recruits students who are first-generation "exclamation point," meaning that no one in their extended family (aunts, uncles, cousins) or in their neighborhoods has graduated from college. For these students, as for those assisted in previous generations by the Morrill Act and the GI Bill, higher education is the pathway to the middle class. Higher education is also the access road to full participation in a democratic society. Every citizen deserves high-quality preparation in critical thinking and communication. That is simply another way of saying that higher education can amplify the voice of every educated citizen. Higher education transforms students' lives—and higher education may be the only pathway to this transformation.

Our work at GSU is informed philosophically by the principle that low-income, first-generation students deserve high-quality bachelor's degrees with a strong foundation in critical thinking and communication. GSU requires freshmen to be full-time and to take at least three classes with the same group of students. These learning communities are organized around the following themes: civic engagement, global citizenship, and sustainability. The cohorts remain together through the first semester of sophomore year, giving students an opportunity to explore a wide choice of majors, including those in the liberal arts. Our mantra is mission before major, helping students to identify their goals before choosing a field of study.

Freshman classes are capped at 30 students, and freshman composition is limited to 18. All freshman courses are taught by full-time, experienced, and dedicated faculty members. That last point is truly revolutionary and disruptive. This serious attention to foundation courses should be emulated by universities across the country. PhD programs in English and the humanities should prepare scholar/teachers for this serious approach to praxis (more on that in chapter 5).

Students and their parents may *say* that what they want from college is merely a degree. But the degree either will not be attained or will be meaningless without the substance and quality that come from engaged learning. Credentials without quality are empty. Whether the student is inspired by the elite peer group attending Harvard or by a professor teaching English composition at GSU, *quality* is defined by mentoring, curricular coherence, and student involvement.

We also know a great deal today about how to achieve these definitive characteristics of successful higher education, braiding equity and quality together. But the first step for students is to convince them that they really can afford college. First-generation exclamation point students need information and guidance on college financial literacy. Many students think that *financial aid* means only loans, and that scholarships—money you don't have to pay back—are only for athletes. At the fall 2014 White House Summit, First Lady Michelle Obama called on university presidents to find better ways to partner with high school guidance counselors. In urban schools these counselors are responsible for advising hundreds of students. They can't do it alone.

GSU is developing courses in master's degree programs for high school guidance counselors to improve their abilities to advise students in preparing for college, both academically and financially. We are also investigating additional avenues to prepare low-income families to encourage college attendance without fear of crushing debt. We have offered free courses to parents of infants and preschoolers in our Family Development Center on financial planning for their young children's college attendance. Universities everywhere can follow suit by establishing a Parent University with these and other courses.

College Goal Sunday, which brings together community resources to encourage completion of the Free Application for Federal Student Aid (FAFSA) form, should be a high-profile event everywhere. In many states, on the Sunday after the Super Bowl, college and university employees accept invitations from churches, Boys' and Girls' Clubs, and other community organizations to set up computers and assist families on the spot in filling out the FAFSA form. Now that families can use the previous year's Internal Revenue Service tax form to fill out the FAFSA in October, I hope that states will establish a statewide activity every fall—post–World Series Sunday, perhaps. Throughout the year, every one of our financial aid employees must be counselors, first and foremost, encouraging students to take on only the loans that they absolutely need for their studies, not for a new automobile or mortgage payments. Counselors must explain to students that full-time study is more economical than part-time, and that full-time means 15 credits per semester (15 to Finish), not quitting their jobs.

It's a fact that most students work, but we must never lower standards because students are busy. Instead, let's find ways to help students integrate their working lives with their studies. If students are working, let us say, in the fast-food industry, then we have a responsibility to help them to connect what they are experiencing in customer service with college courses in psychology, sociology, communications, and marketing. Student employees may not realize it, but their fast-food experience is also teaching them something about the supply chain. It's essential for universities to help students make these connections. Federal work–study funds should be used strategically. At GSU, faculty and administrators compete for work–study students by developing learning experiences, progressively designed from freshman to senior year. GSU strategically allocates work–study funds, waivers, and scholarships to make it possible for students to graduate without unmanageable debt. We also charge the lowest tuition and fees in the Chicago area.

Of course, some changes in federal policy would help: a simplified FAFSA form, the pending return of summer Pell Grants, and a change in the federal mandate about loan availability. Those changes would allow us to counsel students more effectively.

But even with improved financial literacy for lower-income students, some education writers have asked whether the United States can afford to provide mentoring and high-quality liberal education to its low-income citizens. My response is that we cannot afford not to.

In *The End of College: Creating the Future of Learning and the University of Everywhere,* Kevin Carey (2015) describes an untenable future. He predicts that most universities will go out of business except for "15 to 50" traditional, elite, liberal arts colleges, attended, of course, by the economically privileged. Carey asserts that the education available there is simply too expensive for mass consumption, in other words, for inclusivity. The general population will enjoy the "University of Everywhere," which will provide "abundant and free" information in massive open online courses (MOOCs).

As we discuss in chapter 1, it is true that never in the history of the planet has information been more readily available. But information exchange is not education. Now more than ever students must evaluate information, seek connections, and apply facts to decisions. If teaching critical thinking is expensive, just think how expensive it is *not* to teach critical thinking.

We must shape the future so that we do not create a stratified society. Well-meaning reformers are already suggesting that two-year technical education is enough for low-income students—other people's children. But in the same breath these same reformers ask for advice about getting their own kids into Princeton.

I'm not arguing against technical education. A two-year, hands-on technical program could be the on-ramp to an empowering educational pathway. GSU has long experience in offering the inverted baccalaureate—allowing students to build on two-year community college career/technical programs with strong general education in the junior and senior years. The fact remains that in the twenty-first century, two years of technical education may be a good beginning, but it's not enough. We cannot settle for training students for a first job—one that might disappear three years later. I remember that several of my classmates in the inner-city Philadelphia high school that I attended took certificate courses to become keypunch operators. Without preparation for a changing society, where are those keypunch operators today? And then there is the favorite line of misguided politicians: We need welders, not philosophers. That catchphrase is countered by advice from actual welders. An Illinois educator recently met with welders who reported that the physical act of welding is now being done by robotics. Today's welders must be problem solvers and creative thinkers—capacities often associated with, guess what, philosophy.

Without mentoring and high-quality, engaged education for our citizens, we will create a dystopia: a shrinking and ultimately disappearing middle class, a stratified society, and civil unrest. We cannot permit the inequities of the future to be worse than the inequalities of the past. Advanced technology will undoubtedly be highly significant as the twenty-first century moves forward. But we must not allow technological sophistication to create an underclass of automatons—unemployed automatons.

Experts in the digital revolution agree that education must focus on uniquely human capacities. Andrew McAfee, a digital research scientist at MIT, and Erik Brynjolfsson (Brynjolfsson & McAfee, 2012), a professor at MIT, who both authored *Race Against the Machine: How the Digital Revolution Is Accelerating Innovation,*

Driving Productivity, and Irreversibly Transforming Employment and the Economy, and Frank Levy and Richard J. Murnane (n.d.), authors of *Dancing With Robots,* counsel against merely technical education and argue for the necessity of liberal and civic learning for all students. Levy and Murnane call for a new emphasis on "the foundational skills in problem-solving and communication that computers don't have" (p. 4). They do not castigate the schools for deficiencies in teaching these skills but instead point out the "increased complexity of foundational skills needed in today's economy." Even blue-collar jobs, auto mechanics, for example, are "dependent on one's ability to problem solve and communicate" (p. 4).

Brynjolfsson and McAfee (2012) point out that humans have the advantage over computers in goal formation, learning transfer, creativity, motivating others, empathy, and negotiation. They go on to say that computers can liberate us from tasks based on information so that we can concentrate on building a better civilization, infused with the arts and humanities—a new Athens, as it were. In their terms, whereas ancient Athens depended on slave labor, twenty-first-century citizens can depend on computers to do menial tasks, while human society creates a new Golden Age of liberal learning.

Let's consider the implications of Brynjolfsson and McAfee's points for transforming American higher education. We will achieve their vision only through strategy, action, and leadership. We cannot abandon lower-income students to technology-based instruction leading only to first jobs. We must braid equity and quality together, and we must commit ourselves to doing it now.

Lower-income, first-generation students deserve choices. I'm pleased to see that elite, highly selective universities, like my alma mater the University of Pennsylvania, deliberately recruit low-income students and offer full scholarships. Truth be told, wealthy institutions are better able than state flagships to help students graduate without debt. It's important for students to know about these opportunities as early as possible in their K–12 education. Michelle Obama's (2014) plea in her speech at the White House Summit on higher education to work with high school guidance counselors is highly pertinent to defuse the myth of the unaffordability of the Ivy League and other private institutions. Media sound bites seldom communicate to families that the richer the school, the more likely that high-achieving, low-income students will have full expenses covered. And for some students, highly selective colleges and universities are the right choice. But not for others.

The fact remains that many low-income students are, for various reasons, place bound. Their families depend on them for help with younger children or with aging family members. They have jobs they don't want to lose. The idea of leaving their peer group for a faraway rich person's school is not imaginable. Some will aspire to enter their state's flagship research university, but most will begin at community colleges or matriculate directly at regional public universities—those institutions that are members of AASCU.

GSU is an AASCU institution. From our founding in 1969, we have been committed to providing a high-quality education to underserved students: first-generation exclamation point, returning adults, and veterans. As we transformed GSU from upper division to comprehensive, we planned strategically to build in the special benefits of a multigenerational student body. We work to make tangible our ethos as a family campus, avoiding silos wherever we can. The student senate, for example, prepared for the admission of freshmen by rewriting their bylaws for inclusivity. The result is that undergraduates and graduate students of all ages interact productively in shared governance. In the classroom and in co-curricular activities, younger students tell us how much they appreciate the perspectives of older students, who, for example, were adults on September 11, 2001, and can narrate and reflect upon their experiences. Older students value the fresh perspectives and social media savvy of the younger students.

In the fall of 2014, our 42-year-old student senate vice president heard that some freshmen were so comfortable in Prairie Place, our student residence (fully equipped with Wi-Fi, cable, and kitchens), that they were not regularly attending class. He decided to knock on doors and say, "I just want you to know that if you don't attend class, you will flunk out. Don't worry, though. GSU will be there for you when you are 42, like me, but it will be much harder. Go to class." The Center for Civic Engagement, the International Culture Organization, and other co-curricular activities bring the generations together. They also work counter to ethnic group segmentation.

GSU's student body is 50% students of color, and 52% of undergraduates are eligible for Pell Grants. We have a sizeable enrollment of international students, most pursuing master's degrees. We plan strategically for students to engage with each other across lines of age, race, ethnicity, and national origin. The cohort model that requires students as freshmen and first-semester sophomores to take at least three classes with the same group of students encourages friendship bonds across social barriers. Student government and clubs bring together students of various ages and ethnicities to work together on projects. Leadership training seminars, some for men, some for women, some for all, are cross-cutting strategies to achieve real diversity education. Themes uniting each freshman cohort—civic engagement, global citizenship, and sustainability—carry forward to Prairie Place, involving freshmen, upper-division undergraduates, and graduate students. Intercollegiate athletics focused on student-athletes, NAIA not NCAA, bring students together as players and fans. Finally, we are wary of permitting fraternities and sororities on campus because, whatever their benefits, they have the potential to divide students.

Creating environments where students learn from diversity takes strategy and effort. Just so, connecting liberal education and career planning does not happen by itself. We work strategically to counter the erroneous assumption that low-income students should be educated narrowly for a first job, without sufficient preparation for fast-moving changes in twenty-first-century employment. We do not, however, believe that liberal arts courses automatically convey abilities in the critical thinking and problem-solving essential for students' long-term career goals. We must teach students to transfer these abilities from one context to another that might look radically different. Analyzing character and voice in a short story may involve exactly the same skills as analyzing character and voice in a video of a focus group discussion of product branding. But we must structure experiences for students to make that intellectual transfer.

GSU's first-generation exclamation point college students are especially vulnerable to assuming that they must major in something that sounds like a job. Most students are unaware that all majors—whether they sound like a job or not—can lead to lifetime gainful employment and, in many cases, opportunities for advancement and leadership. Faculty members teaching majors in the arts, humanities, and social sciences that don't sound like careers need help in teaching students to transfer skills from the classroom to employment settings. Students need guidance and practice in this transfer. In fact, research shows that teaching for transfer is by far the most challenging part of teaching. In chapter 8, we explore how the Center for the Junior Year (CJY) assists faculty members and students in connecting liberal education and careers.

Teaching for the transfer of liberal education capacities to other contexts is not in conflict with the idea that liberal arts study is worthy for its own sake. The eternal questions of life—Why are we here? What defines *good* and *evil*? How do we create a just society?—will always be illuminated by the liberal arts. Exploring those questions is so important that we cannot deny the opportunity to do so to lower-income students. Braiding together equity and quality may necessitate some emphasis on liberal education as an on-ramp to careers, while, at the same time, students are educated in life pathways. We are influenced by Mount Holyoke College's (n.d.) commitment to connecting liberal arts courses with experiential learning. Twenty-first-century higher education requires breaking down conventional dichotomies between learning for its own sake and learning for careers and responsible citizenship. *Reflection* is the key word. When students reflect on their experiences, they will be better prepared to understand human life and to find fulfillment in all their activities. The University of Iowa's (n.d.) program to connect work and study is called Iowa GROW® (Guided Reflection on Work).

At small private colleges and at public universities, liberal education is available to all students in their general education requirements. To braid equity and quality together, colleges and universities must give special attention to the design and teaching of these foundation-level courses, which, I would argue, are the most important courses in the curriculum. I would go even further by saying that the freshman year in college is one of the three most transformative years in human life, the other two being an infant's first year and a child's first-grade experience. Because of the high, lifelong significance of freshman courses, at GSU these courses are taught exclusively by our most dedicated full-time faculty members. This book encourages all colleges and universities to take first-year courses seriously as early opportunities to transform students from passive recipients of information to active thinkers.

GSU's first-year program requires all students to complete the general education–liberal arts courses mandated in the Illinois Articulation Initiative (IAI). The state legislature established this general education list with the goal of easing student transfer from the community colleges to the universities. Although I am generally opposed to political bodies legislating curriculum, the IAI made it easier for GSU to design a core curriculum of general education courses (English composition, communications, social science, natural science, etc.). The IAI describes these courses broadly enough so that GSU faculty could enrich them from within, making them interactive and stimulating. The faculty used the infusion model to incorporate ethics, citizenship, and art into instruction. (See chapter 4 for further discussion of the infusion model.)

Braiding equity and quality together in the first year must involve close cooperation between academic programs and student services. The first-year seminar, required of all students and taught by faculty from all disciplines on a variety of themes that fulfill a humanities requirement, is an example of collaboration. In addition, support teams are assigned to each student learning community. These teams of career advisers, writing tutors, peer mentors, and psychological counselors come to the students, rather than requiring the students to search for help in disparate offices. In early October, student services, working closely with faculty members, sponsors Save Your Semester, a program that reaches out to students whose transition to university life has been especially challenging. The assignment of midterm grades provides additional opportunities to assist students while there is still time to help.

Philosophically, GSU designs its activities based on a strengths model rather than on a deficit model. Influenced by the research of Shaun Harper and validating information from Gallup, GSU focuses on identifying student strengths and then building upon them. GSU's director of WAC, Kerri Morris, talks about "meeting students where they are." Building on strengths cannot be trivial or falsely flattering. In fact, it is more difficult to identify strengths, which usually go deep, than to notice deficiencies that are usually on the surface. (See further discussion of the strengths model in chapter 6.)

Braiding equity and quality together also involves opening up never-imagined experiences for first-generation exclamation point students. Most of these students are place bound. Many have never traveled much, either domestically or internationally. Even those whose families have emigrated from foreign countries are reluctant to travel once they arrive because of finances or visa restrictions. GSU's mission states explicitly that we are educating students "with the knowledge, skills, and confidence to succeed in a global society" (www.govst.edu/vision2020). Given the circumstances, we seek to provide international education in a variety of ways. Faculty members bring international perspectives to all parts of the curriculum. They incorporate brief, affordable study-abroad experiences into courses. The College of Business, for example, incorporated a two-week study trip to China and invited students from all majors to participate. The study trip was subsidized in part by donors and in part by student activity fees. Similarly, undergraduate and graduate students participate in alternative spring breaks; for example, they travel to Puerto Rico to do service projects. Upon returning to campus, the students make lively and well-attended presentations. I was delighted to hear from all alternative spring breakers that they now wish to study Spanish. Motivating foreign language study is more powerful than requiring it.

International study, even for short periods, opens up students' views of a closed society. Broadening students' perspectives is essential to democracy and to global understanding. To encourage international thinking for all domestic students, including many who cannot take advantage even of our modified study abroad opportunities, GSU recruits international students. It's a special experience for a student who grew up in Chicago Heights to live in Prairie Place next door to a student who grew up in Hyderabad. The student from India also has the educational opportunity to understand U.S. culture from the inside. GSU encourages meaningful interaction in many ways, through the living/learning commitment in the residence halls; through informal athletic competitions; and, most significantly, through the International Culture Organization. Illinois students, who make up at least 40% of the club, plan activities with international students. Some of these activities celebrate worldwide customs like the International Fashion Show, and some involve international students in U.S. cultural activities, like Major League Baseball.

Braiding together equity and quality and preparing students for success in a global society also involves introducing students to opportunities for highly prestigious fellowships for international study, such as Rhodes, Marshall, Truman, and Fulbright. Most first-generation students have never heard of these fellowships, and regional public universities do not have strong traditions of student success in attaining these prizes. Again, it takes action, strategy, and leadership to open up these opportunities. At both UAA and GSU, I asked the honors program to introduce freshmen to the competitive availability of these fellowships. I'm proud to say that before I left UAA, two students had received Fulbright scholarships, and one student was a finalist for the Rhodes scholarship. We are working toward even greater success at GSU.

We have talked about some daunting challenges in this chapter: braiding together equity and quality; thinking strategically about high tech and high touch; and educating for human excellence—for those tasks that only humans, not machines, can do. We have said that these challenges require action, strategy, and leadership at all levels. For true transformation, university presidents must motivate broad-based ownership and leadership. Changes must be evident in the institution's infrastructure, so that the transformation outlives any single presidential administration.

During their tenure, presidents themselves have three major powers to bring about transformational change: final authority on the budget, final authority on personnel decisions, and the microphone. Presidents must use each power carefully, strategically, and effectively. Final authority on the budget means guiding the campus through highly participatory exercises in resource reallocation strategies and then being willing to make the tough decisions. Final authority on personnel decisions means respecting shared governance and traditions of faculty judgment over the hiring and promotion of colleagues as well as enforcing quality standards and protecting employees from bullying and cronyism. It means ensuring that job descriptions for new hires include a statement of university values. Because of the Illinois budget crisis (more on that later), for several years every faculty and staff hire, new or replacement, required presidential approval. The campus grapevine recommended that the best way to gain presidential approval for a hire—any hire—was to demonstrate that the candidate loved freshmen. I have to say that the grapevine, usually wrong, was absolutely right that time. When we returned hiring authority to vice presidents and deans, I wrote the following:

I am confident that any new GSU hire will be committed to our values, including a strong freshman program taught by full-time faculty members; a philosophy of instruction based on connecting with students' strengths; flexibility; team-work; and research-based decision-making.

This quoted memo illustrates what may be the most significant presidential power—the microphone. Whether in speeches, meetings, hallway conversations, or memos, the president's voice is amplified throughout the campus. It's our responsibility and our challenge to use all the powers endowed by the presidential position to transform our campuses into places that braid together equity and quality.

4

ACROSS THE CURRICULUM AND ACROSS THE CAMPUS

The Infusion Model

Writing Across the Curriculum (WAC) is a generative movement that has fundamentally transformed the way we think about both writing and curriculum, and I am proud to be considered one of its founders. Before WAC, linear thinking dominated curriculum planning, exemplified by the impossible expectation that the English department would teach writing once and for all in a first-year course, freeing the rest of the faculty to teach pure content—whatever that is. This linear model also applied to constructing major academic programs by the accumulation of courses and to developing new curricular plans by adding courses— no transformation required, physical change, not chemical change. The underlying assumption is that anything important to student learning deserves a new, distinctive course, or several courses, titled and constructed to cover that subject area. Critical thinking, problem-solving, citizenship, numeracy, artistic sensibility, anything significant, it was thought, deserved to be covered in separate syllabi. Covering material is related to the epistemology of information exchange. "Uncovering material," a phrase coined by Berkeley professor Donald McQuade (personal communication, n.d.), is characteristic of the infusion model and transformational change. WAC was the first major example of infusion and integration—hallmarks of twenty-first-century instruction and scholarship.

41

A brief historical description of WAC is in order. In 1976, Nancy Martin's publication of James Britton's work with the British Schools Council Project, *Writing and Learning Across the Curriculum*, seemed revolutionary. Today, the fundamental idea that it takes a campus to teach a writer is widely acknowledged, although, we must admit, not universally practiced. A minor example: In the 1970s and 1980s, it was radical in an English composition course to include American Psychological Association (APA) documentation as an option rather than the Modern Language Association (MLA) style familiar to English professors. Today, every composition handbook presents multiple forms of documentation, all easily formatted digitally. But the major difference between then and now is understanding writing, not as a separate entity, but as something that must be integrated into all courses. Freshman composition is necessary to establish a foundation, but every course can and should reinforce writing capabilities.

I remember the artless innovation of the late 1970s and early 1980s. Today, I continue to be inspired by a poster on my office wall—the artist's proof for the 1983 Beaver College conference in Philadelphia on writing in the humanities, featuring E.M. Forster's (1910) famous epigraph to *Howards End*, "Only Connect." This conference was the culmination of a project funded by the NEH, titled A National Dissemination Program for Writing in the Humanities, the second of 3 funded programs based at Beaver College (now Arcadia University) that helped to change the culture of higher education by institutionalizing WAC. The first Beaver College NEH initiative was funded in 1977, the same year that the Endowment expanded the Berkeley/Bay Area Writing Project into the National Writing Project (NWP). That year the NWP had 14 sites in 6 states. Today the NWP has nearly 200 sites in all 50 states. While not specifically using the term *writing across the curriculum* or *WAC*, the NWP for the last 4 decades has promoted the infusion of writing into all courses and endeavors, as described on the 2017 NWP website under the phrase "Writing is Essential." "Writing is essential to communication, learning, and citizenship. It is the currency of the new workplace and global economy. Writing helps us convey ideas, solve problems, and understand our changing world. Writing is a bridge to the future" (www.nwp.org/cs/public/print/doc/about.csp).

The NEH is the unsung hero of the infusion model. The NEH funded the NWP, the Beaver College transformation, and the dissemination of WAC principles through institutes at Beaver College and the National Board of Consultants. More than that, the NEH gave its imprimatur to writing as fundamental to the humanities. Before 1977, funding agencies, teacher preparation programs, and classroom teachers defined *writing* as a skill, like carpentry, cooking, or poker playing. Like most skills, the only thing that counted was the final product, with the highest level of achievement considered an art. But writing is more than a finished product. Writing is a complex capacity integrally related to learning and thinking. Without aspiring to artistry, people can write effectively in a variety of settings. In fact, the connection to artistry—the writing of fiction or poetry—intimidates those not majoring in English or aspiring to be the next Toni Morrison.

This conventional English department approach to writing instruction created writer's block in countless students. In 1977, Janet Emig published a seminal article, "Writing as a Mode of Learning." This article was transformational in establishing writing as more than merely transactional, more than something to be covered by the English department in a single course. Emig demonstrated that writing infused across the curriculum promoted greater learning within the disciplines, transcending the accumulation of information to the creation of knowledge and the possibility of wisdom. At the same time, writing integrated as a means of learning increased students' fluency, actually improving transactional communication.

Also in 1977, truly an *annus mirabilis*, Mina Shaughnessy published *Errors and Expectations: A Guide for the Teacher of Basic Writing*. This widely influential book was a major breakthrough. It treats the errors of novice writers not as ignorance, but as windows to their thought processes. The book was the culmination of work done over the previous several years at CUNY to address the needs of students entering college under open admissions—a social experiment designed to empower and educate underprepared students.

Mina Shaughnessy transformed my professional life in San Francisco at the 1975 MLA conference in a talk titled "Diving In," a precursor to her 1977 book. Among the many revolutionary concepts in "Diving In" and *Errors and Expectations* was the recognition of writing as a complex process directly related to thinking and learning. Shaughnessy was an early advocate for WAC. She wrote in *Errors and Expectations*:

> Ways ought to be found to increase students' involvement with writing across the curriculum. This does not mean simply persuading more teachers in other subjects to require term papers but making writing a more integral part of the learning process in all courses. Writing is, after all, a learning tool as well as a way of demonstrating what has been learned. (p. 87)

Shaughnessy's call for making writing "a more integral part of the learning process" is the essence of WAC and the infusion model. *Errors and Expectations* was a landmark work in making college composition a scholarly field.

At that 1975 MLA meeting, I met Harriet Sheridan, dean of Carleton College, who was then serving as acting president of that prestigious liberal arts college in Minnesota. After Mina Shaughnessy's talk, Dean Sheridan and I were both on a cable car headed for Fisherman's Wharf, and she heard me extolling "Diving In." We formed a bond. She then told me about Carleton's approach to writing: faculty rhetoric seminars and students learning to become rhetoric fellows. I returned to Beaver College with The Carleton Plan for WAC. This plan inspired Beaver College's first NEH grant, received in July 1977, "A program to strengthen the humanities at Beaver College through an emphasis on instruction in writing and reading by all faculty."

The 1977 NEH grant made it possible for Beaver College to invite scholars to conduct workshops for faculty from across the disciplines. The idea for the faculty workshop has its roots in the 1974 and 1975 Carleton College faculty rhetoric seminars, the brainchild of Harriet Sheridan, who is in many ways the godmother of WAC. We invited Sheridan to be the first faculty workshop leader at Beaver College. In January 1977, Dean Sheridan communicated undeniably that we were embarking on a serious enterprise by selecting Aristotle's *Rhetoric* for the first reading assignment.

The list of subsequent Beaver College workshop leaders reads like the all-stars of late 1970s scholarship in rhetoric and composition—Edward P.J. Corbett, Linda Flower and Dick Hayes, Donald McQuade, Richard Young, E.D. Hirsch, Fred Crews, Nancy Sommers, Lynn Bloom. (We invited Mina Shaughnessy, who was gracious and supportive but too ill to participate.) Our guests were not WAC scholars—the field did not yet exist. We were creating something new together. We invited multiple experts to present multiple points of view. No single perspective prevailed. Beaver College faculty members had to assess how Flower and Hayes's exploration of writing and cognitive psychology connected with Corbett's scholarship on Greek rhetoric, how Sommers's research on faculty responses to student writing matched up with Bloom's perspectives on autobiography, and how any or all of it connected to transformation at Beaver College.

Most leaders led the faculty workshop for four summer days, leaving the fifth day for our own reflection, synthesis, and application of concepts. We did not expect outside experts to sell prepared programs. The success of WAC at Beaver College depended on the creativity and ownership of our own faculty developing applications that made sense in our own context and for our own students. Curriculum change depends on scholarly exchange among faculty members.

The faculty workshop itself became an important legacy of WAC. Before the Carleton rhetoric seminars, nothing like it had existed. The workshops were not committee meetings, graduate seminars, or parties, but somehow they combined the best features of all three. Writing workshops were settings for communal scholarship applied to pedagogic problems. Most important, workshops were politically and intellectually nonhierarchical. Department heads and full professors worked as equals with untenured assistant professors. English and math instructors discussed writing as a learning process. In an atmosphere of participatory transformation, everyone's expertise was valuable; everyone's questions were generative.

Today, the faculty workshop—on a variety of subjects—is taken for granted as a vehicle for change. In the late 1970s, I must confess, WAC leaders—Toby Fulwiler and Art Young, then at Michigan Tech; Barbara Walvoord, then at Central College; and myself—did not realize that we were creating a new format for faculty interaction, creativity, and transformation. We were just doing what seemed reasonable and potentially effective. As young crusaders with no institutional power, we stumbled on a format that fostered change—and it still does.

The writing workshops promoted reflection by faculty members on their own writing processes, connecting students' struggles with their own. These experiences underlined writing as a process, sometimes intended solely as a learning tool, sometimes as a step toward going public with a finished project. One of the early Beaver College faculty workshops was led by the editor of a scholarly journal. After discussing student writing in the morning, faculty members were invited to make individual appointments in the afternoon with the editor to discuss their own work in progress. This experience made vital connections between students and professors as writers, illuminating a continuum from novice to expert; promoting empathy with students' difficulties; and communicating experientially the idea of writing as a complex, recursive process.

This connection between students and faculty members as writers, along with many later workshop activities, resulted in doing more than infusing writing in courses across the curriculum. Faculty members were ready to integrate writing processes by assigning and commenting on drafts. If faculty scholars need constructive commentary on work in progress, then it makes sense that student writers benefit from questions and suggestions on drafts. Treating students as writers, rather than as pupils waiting for final grades, has many implications. Faculty members learn to act as coaches, to take student work seriously and to have high standards, but to withhold judgment. Students are encouraged to act like writers, learning how to request help at appropriate stages in the process and to acknowledge that assistance on an acknowledgments page, as authors do when they go public.

Understanding writing as an often messy process for experts as well as for novices led to other Beaver College innovations. The Writing Clinic, suggesting that student writing was sick and needed treatment, was transformed into the Writing Center, staffed by peer writing consultants. The idea was that writers at all levels of experience need readers of work in progress. Students can be trained to read drafts and ask generative questions. Novice writers get help; more advanced student writers learn how to motivate better writing without becoming an editor or a coauthor (a very useful career skill for future supervisors). Inspired by Harriet Sheridan's rhetoric fellows at Carleton College, Beaver College brought the peer writing consultants out of the Writing Center and into class-rooms. Faculty members could request writing consultants, who had excelled in the course in a previous semester, to read drafts of student writing and provide comments and questions. These peers did not grade final products but instead guided less experienced students in course-based writing and learning. In the 1980s, when Harriet Sheridan became dean of the College at Brown University, she established the nationally recognized and emulated Writing Fellows Program there.

The Beaver College program developed original versions of what were later to become twenty-first-century innovations: writing as a process, drafting across the curriculum, peer review of work in progress, transformation of writing clinics into writing centers, port-folios (not "e" at the time), writing fellows, learning communities, and freshman composition as the foundation for WAC. In essence, WAC moved the sage from the stage by encouraging instructors to guide from the side.

Learning communities today have their roots in Beaver College's *course clusters*, establishing thematic linkages for connected thinking for students and professors. The first Beaver College course cluster brought together nineteenth-century British literature, nineteenth-century British history, and evolution. The common thread was Charles Darwin. Students were invited to do drafting across the curriculum, submitting a draft to one instructor for com-ments and then the finished paper to another instructor for a grade that would count in two courses. Some students drafted and revised with all three courses and instructors in the mix. The original pur-pose for the course clusters was to provide an ongoing structure for faculty development, with colleagues reading each other's com-ments on student papers and consulting about what constitutes suc-cessful writing. This original goal was fulfilled, but it became clear that the students were gaining enormously from experiencing con-nected thinking in action and seeing it modeled by their professors. The Beaver College course clusters of 1978 led to the GSU learning communities and thematic cohorts of 2018.

The Beaver College transformation, based on innovations devel-oped by an engaged faculty committed to the integration of teaching and scholarship, went beyond new approaches to writing. In 1981, with the help of a grant from the Fund for the Improvement of Postsecondary Education (FIPSE), Beaver College conducted faculty workshops to integrate critical thinking and problem-solving into the curriculum. No doubt, this new emphasis necessarily involved writing, but the different focal point shifted attention to the conceptual establishment of the infusion model.

In the early 1980s, in addition to developing the infusion model beyond writing per se and consolidating and institutionalizing WAC on campus, Beaver College extensively disseminated WAC nationally. Beaver College faculty members responded to numerous invitations from universities, colleges, and school districts to assist in establishing programs according to principles developed at Beaver College. In 1980, NEH funded a major grant to disseminate WAC. During the summers of 1981 and 1982, teams of college and secondary school instructors from various geographical regions—from El Paso, Texas to San Juan, Puerto Rico—assembled in the Philadelphia suburbs on the Beaver College campus to study the infusion of writing into courses across the curriculum and to discuss political strategies to use back home.

This dissemination project was designed to create teams of change-makers. The regional teams included an English professor, a professor from another discipline, and a high school teacher from the same region. For three weeks, team members studied with Beaver College faculty members and with specially invited national scholars. The teams also worked on implementation plans for the next academic year. The plans were required to go beyond campus writing reform to reach out to local feeder high schools (thus the membership of a high school teacher on the team). During the fourth and final week of the workshop, the institute hosted a small, invitational conference, featuring team presentations of future plans. In the audience were senior administrators (deans or above), whose committed attendance had been part of the competitive application process for team participation in the institute. During the subsequent academic year, NEH funding supported consultative site visits to institute campuses by Beaver College workshop leaders to assist with implementation. The 1983 conference on writing in the humanities brought together the teams from the summers of 1981 and 1982, as well as other academics interested in implementing

WAC. The institute teams presented the outcomes of their implementation plans.

NEH was impressed with our results and subsequently funded a project focused on Philadelphia-area teams of secondary school teachers participating in summer seminars on WAC. The umbrella theme of these seminars was "the teacher," emphasizing the role of the president of the United States, starting with Thomas Jefferson, as the Teacher in Chief, setting the national framework for learning. Integrating WAC with complex historical themes illustrated for the teachers the effectiveness of connecting writing and learning in their classrooms.

The late 1970s and early 1980s was also the time when NEH conducted one of the most cost-effective and powerful programs in higher education: the National Board of Consultants. The idea was simple. In a brief application—5 pages or so—a college or university outlined a problem focusing on improving humanities instruction in its setting. NEH then identified a member of the National Board of Consultants (made up mainly of project directors for current and past NEH projects) to design a series of visits to address the goals of the proposal. Janice Litwin, during her 12-year tenure at NEH (1972–1984), created the program and then made matches worthy of Dolly Levi.

Two of my NEH consultancies, one at El Centro Community College (Dallas, Texas) and one at Pacific Lutheran University (Tacoma, Washington), led to enduring WAC programs. Pacific Lutheran became the leader of a Pacific Northwest Regional Consortium on WAC. The National Board of Consultants in general facilitated transformational change in higher education. NEH would be well advised to reestablish this board and make small grants for consultation available once again.

The NEH institutes and the National Board of Consultants illustrate the following important principles of transformational change that hold true today:

- Bringing in outside expertise can serve as a flash point for important campus conversations.
- Experts, however, should not be permitted to sell entire plans.

- Engaging faculty members in an inquiry mode results in innovative thinking.
- Collaborative learning and working in teams yield new ideas that might not emerge from solitary thought.
- It's essential to create safe spaces where no one is cut off prematurely because the idea sounds silly or "we tried it before, and it doesn't work."
- It's important to provide opportunities for immediate application to try out new ideas.
- Follow-up is crucial to apply and assess what has been developed.

By the mid-1980s, through the NEH institutes and the NEH National Board of Consultants, WAC, the original infusion model, had traction across the country. Coast-to-coast dissemination was helped greatly in the mid-1980s and 1990s by a series of national faculty workshops sponsored by the University of Chicago under the general title of Writing and Thinking. Carol Geary Schneider, later to become the long-term and transformative president of AAC&U, was then University of Chicago's impresario for extended education. By good luck and timely intellectual matchmaking by a fellow FIPSE director, Schneider and I met and infused writing into the originally planned cognitive emphasis of the Chicago conferences. In addition to University of Chicago scholars Wayne Booth and Joe Williams and a living bibliography of innovative cognitive psychologists, the Chicago conferences invited guest workshop leaders from other universities to work with faculty teams from around the country. These conferences, two per year for nearly a decade, gave the University of Chicago imprimatur to the integral relationship between writing and thinking.

As the new millennium dawned, WAC matured from an innovation on the sidelines to something evident in the mainstream. Writing as a mode of learning was becoming widely accepted and promoted through books and articles suggesting strategies designed to employ informal writing—journals, brief reflections on key issues, summaries of main points, letters written on course topics, and so on. On many campuses the ePortfolio emerged, even before technology fully caught up with the idea. Students were assigned to keep a portfolio of ungraded drafts. They would then review these drafts—sometimes with advice from peers—and then select material for further development and revision.

At an increasing number of colleges and universities, first-year composition students were introduced to a world of shifting contexts, where thinking through the rhetorical situation is fundamental. Textbooks with a WAC framework became widely adopted. Introductory composition courses increasingly transformed understanding of what is fundamental for writers. Before the WAC revolution, surface skills (grammar, punctuation, and spelling) were considered to be basic. Grammar, punctuation, and spelling are undeniably important on finished products because the reader sees them first, but working on the surface is the opposite of foundational. The most enlightened first-year composition courses, including the one now taught at GSU, encompass the following goals:

- Introduce students to writing processes—generating, drafting, and revising—and emphasize the recursive, nonlinear, variable, and complex nature of these procedures.
- Introduce students to the variability of contexts across the curriculum and in situations beyond the campus.
- Introduce students to peer review—how to read and comment constructively on classmates' writing and how to benefit from multiple and often differing comments from peer reviewers.
- Provide numerous opportunities to use writing to learn, resulting in increased fluency and increased learning.
- Introduce students to assessing research, with an emphasis on evaluating online materials.
- Guide students to resources for editing and proofreading (handbooks and online materials), with the expectation of producing successful public documents.

First-year composition courses committed to these goals build a strong foundation for WAC, making it possible for instructors in all fields to reinforce these capacities and to refine students' understanding of the particular thought processes reflected in various disciplines.

When WAC is fully integrated into a campus culture, writing assignments become primary in new course development and existing course revision. Recently, for example, at GSU, we were engaged in discussions about how to implement Michelle Obama's (2014) challenge for universities to do a better job in preparing high school guidance counselors to provide sound, comprehensive advice on selecting and financing a college education. One of the first suggestions was to incorporate an assignment involving the preparation of a presentation to parents, with special consideration of what families without college experiences of their own need to know. When writing assignments have primacy, it's a sure sign that writing is infused across the curriculum.

As we developed a structured, four-year undergraduate curriculum at GSU, we used the WAC example of infusion as a seedbed to fulfill other curricular goals. Our physical campus is integrated with the internationally acclaimed Nathan Manilow Sculpture Park (NMSP). When *New Yorker* art critic Peter Schjeldahl visited the university, he was particularly impressed with the thoughtful attention our buildings and grounds staff paid to carefully maintaining the prairie settings for the great works of sculpture. The infusion of art across the curriculum and across the campus was a natural. "Living in the midst of art" is designed for all students, faculty, and staff to be mindful of the art around them, not only the NMSP but also glass art by Charles Lotton and student and faculty art displayed everywhere on campus. Living in the midst of art includes the performing arts with attention to the integration of community and student productions at our Center for Performing Arts and elsewhere on campus. In the spring of 2017, GSU's theater department performed Shakespeare's *The Tempest* in the NMSP. Faculty members integrate art into their courses. A math instructor, for example, assigns students to compare human proportions to Tony Tasset's monumental statue of a weary Paul Bunyan in the NSMP.

The infusion model is also our vehicle for teaching citizenship. Influenced by *A Crucible Moment: College Learning and Democracy's Future* (National Task Force on Civic Learning and Democratic Engagement, 2012), we are committed to putting "civic learning at the core rather than the periphery" (p. 25). Citizenship across the curriculum means that instructors connect their course work to public policy. Connections need not be complex or fancy, simply what engaged citizens and responsible voters need to think about. In a statistics course, how do candidates for elected office use statistics?

In an education course, what are the pros and cons of standardized testing? In a communications course, what rhetorical devices are candidates using in speeches and debates? In a nursing course, what are the implications of the Affordable Care Act for health care in Illinois and in the nation? This integrated approach is far more effective than adding a separate course on civics. Citizenship across the curriculum creates what *A Crucible Moment* calls "a civic ethos" (p. 14), while making traditional course work more relevant and dynamic.

GSU also infuses career preparation across the curriculum. From freshman year to senior year, students are encouraged to think explicitly about the connection of the classroom and careers. Helping students to transfer learning, particularly in the liberal arts, from the classroom to current and future employment requires explicit instruction. It's important to go beyond proclamations that students in the liberal arts are effective writers, critical thinkers, and communicators. Encouraging students to transfer capacities from one setting to another is probably the most challenging part of teaching. It helps to design specific assignments, demonstrating, for example, that the ability to make constructive suggestions for the revision of a classmate's first draft translates into a necessary supervisory skill— showing an employee how to improve a project rather than taking over the task oneself. The difference in context can make these connections unrecognizable unless they are pointed out.

"Only Connect," says E.M. Forster (1910). The infusion model connects course work and careers, students and academic study, the university and life.

5

EXPLODING THE
HIERARCHICAL FALLACY

The Significance of Foundation-Level Courses

The evidence is mounting. One of the most significant challenges in higher education is inadequate attention to first-year courses. Bowen and McPherson (2016) point to "the deadening effect of too much poor teaching of foundational courses . . . especially among less well-prepared students" (p. viii) as one of the major problems in American higher education.

At the same time, alumni surveys; Gallup (2014) research; and, frankly, common sense indicate that the most important factor in student success is a mentor, usually a faculty member who, from day one, cares about the student. Because college drop-out rates are highest in the first year, it is particularly important that first-year students connect with the professors teaching general education courses, and it is best if these professors are full-time faculty members.

It is difficult for even the most talented part-time instructors to fulfill the mentor role for simple logistical reasons. To make a living, adjuncts spend precious hours on the road driving from one university to another, and even if they keep office hours, they are unavailable for informal interactions in the hallway, in the cafeteria, or at co-curricular activities. Permanent faculty members are present and involved in the life of an institution outside the classroom. And it should go without saying that foundational courses—introductions to the intellectual life of our society—are the least likely candidates for MOOCs or other online, depersonalized approaches.

It is vital to recognize, however, that faculty members teaching foundational courses must be more than mentors. They must be outstanding teachers and scholars. Foundational courses are difficult to teach. Getting to the core of anything is an intellectual challenge. Discovering the foundation without getting stuck on the seductive surface is a job for experts, not novices. The courses themselves must be constructed to motivate active engagement, not passive receptivity. The academy has done embarrassingly little research on what defines the *essential*. Yet, introductory courses are routinely assigned to the least experienced, lowest compensated, and most overworked. Instead, the best minds on campus should be researching intellectual foundations and applying this scholarship to their teaching of first-year courses.

If we are to have real reform in American higher education, first-year courses must be recognized not as requirements to be checked off and done with but as true foundations for higher order thinking and learning. For more than two decades, John Gardner and Betsy Barefoot have done outstanding work in developing conferences and institutes on the first-year experience. Gardner and Barefoot's Institute for Excellence in Undergraduate Education has prepared teams of faculty members and administrators to transform their campuses through heightened attention to the freshman year. Their books have been highly influential in this transformation (Barefoot et al., 2005; Felten, Gardner, Schroeder, Lambert, & Barefoot, 2016). As a consequence, colleges and universities have access to multiple strategies for developing outstanding courses. To build on that work, these courses must be further recognized for their intellectual significance and their inherent possibilities for multidisciplinary scholarship.

Even well-intentioned reformers call only for improved pedagogy rather than seeing foundational education as worthy of serious research as well as expert teaching. Bowen and McPherson's (2016) solution is to develop a "teaching corps" of nontenured faculty members to teach foundational courses. I see their suggestion as much too limited. Instead, I believe in something truly disruptive. Faculty members should be outstanding teachers and first-rate researchers on questions inherent in foundational study. Making these connections depends on redefining and transforming educational hierarchies.

I call it the Maimon Hierarchical Fallacy. If I teach graduate students, and you teach undergraduates, I must be smarter than you. If I teach seniors, and you teach freshmen, I must be smarter than you. This fallacy also applies at levels below college: If I teach sixth grade, and you teach first grade, I must be smarter. The challenges of twenty-first-century education require recognizing and reordering these hierarchies.

Even as we examine and upset hierarchies, we must retain the significance of research to university teaching. Although teachers at all levels should stay up to date in their fields, universities are essentially places for the discovery of knowledge. Research on introductory courses is an important component of that discovery. A group of "only-teachers," set apart from the research mandate of the university, will not earn appropriate respect, and we will be deprived of the necessary knowledge based on *praxis*, a Greek term meaning the intellectual process by which theories are enacted—turned into action.

The Maimon Hierarchical Fallacy has special meaning in my own field of English. Here is the English department version: Those who teach literature are smarter than those who teach composition. Those who write about theory are smarter than those who write about praxis. Those who teach graduate courses are smarter than those who teach composition. These hierarchical fallacies even affect scholarship in PhD programs specializing in rhetoric and composition. It is hard to believe that some theorists in writing think that it is below their dignity to teach composition—and they don't. These full-time faculty members regard teaching the very discipline they are studying as unworthy of their elevated intellects.

They reject praxis and forget another lesson from the Greeks in the story of the wrestler Antaeus. No one could defeat Antaeus because he gained his strength from his mother, the Earth. Whenever he was knocked down, the earth restored him. For scholars of rhetoric and composition, freshman English is the earth. Hercules finally defeated Antaeus by holding him aloft—away from the earth—in the realm of pure theory. Hercules was then able to crush Antaeus to death.

Doctoral programs in English are on a death march. Even so, the goal seems to be to protect the status quo at any cost. The reforms suggested by the MLA Task Force on Doctoral Study in Modern Language and Literature (2014) direct PhD candidates in English to careers outside the academy, as if that would justify retaining the same number of graduate faculty teaching the same number of students in the same kinds of courses.

I am certainly in favor of helping current PhD candidates to explore job opportunities outside the academy, and I support strategic approaches to doing so like those described by Peter Conn (2010). But we cannot continue admitting large numbers of students aspiring to become professors and then after years of study and indebtedness show them alternative careers. My radical suggestion is to prepare PhD candidates in English for jobs *within* the academy through a new emphasis on the intellectual challenge of teaching and doing research on foundational courses like freshman composition. Doing so requires drastic rethinking of PhD preparation to match twenty-first-century epistemology.

The PhD has always required specialization and should continue to do so. But what does *specialization* denote in the twenty-first century? It no longer means the vast accumulation of information. Instead, it means the expertise to create new knowledge. In the field of English that new knowledge encompasses language and literature in all its forms. Deep-seated knowledge in one area should be combined with the flexibility and connected thinking of the generalist. Experts in Shakespeare should be prepared to teach writing, and experts in writing should be excellent at teaching introductory courses in Shakespeare.

Just so, regional public universities and liberal arts colleges need specialists who can also be generalists, professors with focus and with peripheral vision. The better that point is understood, the more PhD candidates in English and in other humanities disciplines will be hired for tenure-track positions at regional public universities and liberal arts colleges and the more students will benefit from top scholars making vital connections across the wide field of language and literature. The academy can encourage scholarship on the complexities of learning to write and to think creatively, critically, and innovatively.

Of course, doctoral professors in the humanities would have to explode their hierarchical, self-perpetuating definition of *success*. If PhD candidates believe that anything other than a tenure-track position at a research university demonstrates their inadequacy, the transformations I suggest can never happen. We need a major cultural shift in priorities, reflected in reallocations in university budgets. We must design more efficient and effective graduate education, freeing resources for investment in foundational programs.

A transformed PhD in English would include some course work in rhetoric and composition, no matter what the student's specialty. Likewise, composition and rhetoric specialists would be prepared to teach introductory courses in literature. Every program would include the study of higher education in the United States, emphasizing the faculty role in shared governance. The absence in PhD programs of serious attention to the institutional role of faculty members leads to the assumption that professors are independent contractors with affiliations to their profession but not to any educational institution. For years, we have been growing our own problems by socializing newcomers into the profession with these false assumptions. We then wonder about contentious relationships between faculty members and administration and the difficulty in encouraging talented faculty members to take on leadership positions. Identifying administration as "the dark side" is a by-product of harmful and false acculturation during PhD preparation.

David Thiele (2016), an associate professor of English at the University of Mount Union, suggests, "Every doctoral student who plans to work in the academy should be required to take a course in higher education." He argues that a course in higher education is foundational to doctoral study and would help create more responsible citizens in the academy. One respondent to Thiele's article, Tracy Mitrano (n.d.), makes an even more important point,

> I agree but for reasons even greater than preparing the candidate professionally. As a historian of higher education, I learned that the history of higher education is the history of the United States at its finest. To read that history is to know something about ourselves, our ideals and our disappointments. And most importantly: why it matters.

Higher education, especially public higher education—the legacy of Thomas Jefferson and the Morrill Act—is increasingly under threat in the United States. It is imperative that faculty members and administrators bring historical perspective to the debate. For that reason alone, it would make sense for every doctoral program to include a required course in higher education. The curriculum change that David Thiele, Tracy Mitrano, and I are suggesting is not a course in pedagogy, although doctoral students need that preparation as well.

Numerous reformers have suggested attention to pedagogy in PhD programs. My own experience with successful approaches to the teaching of college English exemplifies what works. Systematic mentorship can transform PhD candidates into creative teachers. I was lucky enough in my own PhD preparation from 1966 to 1970 at the University of Pennsylvania to be a graduate fellow in a highly structured four-year program. This program for graduate fellows was supported by the Ford Foundation and the National Defense Education Act (NDEA). Wouldn't it be wonderful if the nation could once again see the preparation of English professors as part of our national defense? That could happen if English professors put greater emphasis on preparing students to be critical thinkers and effective writers.

In the first year of the graduate fellows program, we concentrated on course work, including a proseminar, in which we were encouraged to apply the research techniques we were learning to potential topics and questions that might define our dissertations. In the second year, in addition to continued course work, each PhD candidate was assigned full-time observation in a senior professor's classroom with in-depth discussions of class organization and teaching techniques. My mentor lived up to the role. He did not use me as a grader. Instead, he and I both commented on student papers and then discussed our tactics, as well as everything else that might matter in a successful foundational course.

In the third year, fellows taught courses in freshman composition with the ongoing advice of our mentors. The fourth year was devoted to writing the dissertation. Because of the intelligent structure of this Ivy League PhD program in English, I am proud to say that I completed my PhD in 4.5 years, while I was still in my early 20s. The organization of the program, including the built-in mentoring, allowed me to launch an early career, even though, as is almost always the case, life happened during this period. I got married and gave birth to my first child, but I had my PhD in hand.

PhD programs are apprenticeships, and apprenticeships should be well structured and efficient. Four to five years of concentrated study and writing should be sufficient to achieve a PhD in English and in other humanities disciplines. Intense, concentrated study, writing, and teaching mirror the necessary existence of successful professors. The preparatory period should encourage apprentices to balance the demands of academic life.

It's also important to note that successful PhD dissertations, because they are—and should be—apprentice work, are almost never ready for immediate publication in book form. The dissertation is its own genre, subject to the instructional goals of the dissertation committee. Revising the dissertation for publication nearly always requires independence from that committee. On countless occasions, I have advised PhD candidates to finish the dissertation; satisfy the review committee; and later, after the apprenticeship has concluded, turn the dissertation into their own book. Dragging out the apprenticeship for a decade or more makes no sense for the student educationally or economically. The economic advantage has been entirely in the interest of the university, benefitting from (exploiting?) the cheap labor of graduate assistants teaching introductory courses.

I fully recognize that large research universities cannot staff every section of freshman composition with a full-time faculty member as I recommend for regional public institutions and liberal arts colleges. But large research universities can structure the teaching experience in the context of enlightened apprenticeship. One option is to revive and fund the graduate fellows program that I experienced in the late 1960s. Several years later, the University of Pennsylvania pioneered another excellent model for preparing English PhD candidates to teach and value freshman composition. In the 1980s, Robert Lucid, my dissertation supervisor at the University of Pennsylvania, became chair of the English department. He invited me to consult on instituting WAC at Penn. The program we developed, Writing Across the University (WATU), still exists.

As a by-product of that consultation, the University of Pennsylvania established a team approach to teaching freshman composition. Peter Conn, now the Vartan Gregorian Emeritus Professor of English and a professor of education, developed a graduate course, English 886, setting up a system for teams of graduate students to work with senior professors, all of whom taught composition and met to discuss and assess their work. Conn himself, a distinguished scholar in American literature, led a team and encouraged other University of Pennsylvania English professors to join him in this project.

It's worth taking a closer look at English 886, because it's an available model for what is needed today. Conn was a pioneer in breaking down hierarchies. He writes, "The design of each course depends on three acts of premeditated connection: between graduate study and freshman teaching, between the study of composition and the study of literature, between the faculty and graduate students" (Conn, 1982, p. 6). Conn and his graduate student team selected four books—*Huckleberry Finn; The House of Mirth; Winesburg, Ohio;* and *The Great Gatsby*—as the reading list for students in their freshman sections and for intense study and discussion in the graduate seminar. The graduate students were also required to read a number of articles on composition research and the teaching of writing.

Conn's idea—decades ahead of its time—was for the graduate professor and graduate students to become what he terms a genuine *teaching company.* Everyone benefited. The senior professors broke down hierarchies and modeled their own commitment to learning. The graduate students practiced the intersections between literature and composition, teaching and learning, foundational and advanced work. They taught writing as they were doing their own dissertation writing, understanding thereby the complexity of the writing process for expert and novice. Freshmen at the University of Pennsylvania had instructors, whether graduate students or tenured professors, who were taking their novice work seriously and mentoring them as new entrants into the intellectual community.

PhD programs in English at research universities are uniquely qualified to establish these teaching companies. Conn pointed this out in his 1982 article. "What we did," he wrote, "is easily replicable in almost any university setting" (p. 6). One of the graduate student participants reflected on the experience, "English 886 introduced second-year graduate students to the profession of teaching English. Each element of the course contributed to the graduate students' process of discovering an institution" (p. 6).

But English 886 does not exist today. Why didn't this brilliant, scalable approach grow, transforming English PhD programs and the teaching of freshman composition at the University of Pennsylvania and elsewhere? Here is Conn's explanation:

The project did not long survive. It limped along in incrementally diluted versions for several years, after which it was pushed out to sea on an ice floe to expire. Whatever its merits or demerits, like many innovations it suffered from "founder's syndrome." (Personal communication, August 26, 2016)

It's time that good ideas—imperative ideas like this one—find widespread adoption in twenty-first-century research universities. Such programs would prepare future faculty members for employment in a broad range of institutions.

We have other models on which to draw. From 1993 to 2003, the Council of Graduate Schools (CGS) joined with AAC&U, with support from the Pew Charitable Trusts, the National Science Foundation, and the Atlantic Philanthropies, to implement Preparing Future Faculty (PFF) at 45 PhD-granting universities and nearly 300 partner institutions. The idea is transformational: Provide PhD candidates with opportunities to be mentored by faculty members at a variety of colleges and universities with varying missions and diverse student bodies.

In the 1990s, when I led ASU West, my campus happily participated in PFF. I saw firsthand that the program broke down hierarchies; provided eager apprentices to regional universities; and inculcated intellectual flexibility in its participants, students, and mentors. Although PFF still exists under the auspices of the Council of Graduate Programs, the visibility and potential power of the program have diminished substantially. PFF is yet another instance of our already knowing how to improve doctoral education, if we have the will and the courage to reallocate resources—and to eradicate the Maimon Hierarchical Fallacy.

We must move forward with fundamental and sustained reform in PhD programs in the humanities to integrate pedagogy, as well as the history, philosophy, and culture of higher education. This reform requires transformational shifts in university budget allocations, benefiting students at all levels. PhD candidates in the humanities should enter structured doctoral programs like the one I experienced at the University of Pennsylvania. Course work would include a foundational course in higher education and structured pedagogical experiences. Graduate students would begin in their first semester to think about possible dissertation topics and to use papers written for subsequent courses to test questions and approaches for the culminating project. This efficient, brief apprenticeship would prepare PhD recipients for employment at a full range of universities and colleges.

At research universities, the restructuring and greater efficiency of PhD programs would free up resources to invest in foundation-level courses. At regional public universities and liberal arts colleges, the availability of new faculty hires who are both specialists and generalists would enable assigning duties that encompass engaged teaching and scholarship at all levels. At research universities, the goal should be to raise the prestige of teaching and of scholarship applied to first-year courses. At the regional public universities and liberal arts colleges, the goal should be to staff foundation-level courses with full-time professors who take this work seriously from both a teaching and research perspective. For those smaller universities offering master's degrees in the humanities, it's important to streamline those programs with specific goals in mind. These budget reallocations are radical but doable. Do the programs exist primarily so that senior faculty members can teach their literary specialties? Can the master's degrees be revised to offer integrated approaches to the disciplines, potentially with a special focus on educating community college instructors?

At GSU, we have implemented budget reallocations along these lines. We have transformed both undergraduate- and master's-level education in the humanities. Only full-time faculty members teach freshmen, and these faculty members are encouraged to do high-level research connecting theory and practice. These transformations go beyond English and the humanities disciplines.

Foundational courses in math also require radical transformation, and math professors at GSU have embraced those changes. Uri Treisman (Cullinane & Treisman, 2010), Andrew Hacker (2012), and others have written extensively and persuasively on the subject. Treisman argues that the conventional math curriculum, enshrined in most high-stakes standardized tests, assumes that calculus is the appropriate foundation for advanced numeracy. But he and other mathematicians have come to the conclusion that "calculus is a filter that has become a choke-point as the economy becomes more and more technical" (Kaplan, 2013). "By contrast, many of the fundamentals of statistics . . . are broadly useful to people as they make

decisions in their roles as professionals, citizens, and even parents"
(Manyika & Chui, 2013). My personal experience illustrates the
validity of these findings. My Ivy League undergraduate education
did not include calculus, and I have never missed it for a single day.
However, my education did not include formal work in statistics,
and I miss it every day.

Foundational courses in math should be geared to the student's
prospective major, and the statistics track should not be considered
inferior to calculus, thus exploding another hierarchical assumption. Foundational math courses can then highlight relevancy.
From the start, students should understand the essential applications of calculus to science, technology, engineering, and mathematics (STEM) fields. Likewise, courses in introductory statistics
should empower students to make data-driven decisions as scholars
and citizens.

The Maimon Hierarchical Fallacy is directly related to what
Alexander Astin (2016) calls the "higher education pecking order"
(p. 7). His point is that professors, students, and the general public
are acculturated to believe that those universities that admit only
those who are already *smart*, as defined by high school grades and
standardized test scores, are the best institutions. Astin (2016) goes
on to say that "too many of the 1.5 million faculty members who
staff our 4,000-plus institutions of higher learning have come to
value merely *being* smart more than *developing* smartness! . . . Our
country cannot afford to educate only a select segment of its population" (pp. 1–2). The necessity to lead academic change could not
be more vital. We must shift priorities to developing smartness, in
other words preparing professors and transforming institutions to
focus on the value added for each student from freshman year to
graduation.

It is most gratifying to see hierarchies of all kinds exploded at
GSU. Each semester I attend a meeting chaired by GSU's director of general education. The participants are faculty members—all
full-time faculty members—who are teaching in the freshman and
first-semester-sophomore cohorts. These highly interactive meetings are inspiring. They remind me of the WAC workshops of my
youth. Faculty members explore ways to improve the vital connections among their courses. They share strategies for addressing problems. They openly assess what is not working and why.

In my role as listener-in-chief, I am in awe of my colleagues' commitment to students. Faculty members search for additional ways to support first-generation freshmen and sophomores in fulfilling high standards of achievement. Running through my mind is Robert Browning's (1855) famous line, "Ah, but a man's reach should exceed his grasp / Or what's a heaven for?" GSU faculty members are reaching into uncharted intellectual realms so that their students can stretch beyond their comfort zones to imagine and achieve goals they never before perceived.

One point is eminently clear: This work is hard—for students and for professors. It requires creativity, imagination, critical thinking, resilience, and strategy. As the professors reflect on the semester's work, they unanimously agree on the amazing student growth they have witnessed from August to December. GSU faculty members teaching in the freshman and sophomore cohorts do not have the time or energy to perpetuate outdated hierarchies. They are focused on the task of transformation—transforming students' lives and by doing so transforming American higher education. When it's time to go from appreciative listening to using the president's power of the microphone, I say just two words, "Thank you."

6

RETHINKING
REMEDIATION

This chapter is a call for scholars to study remedial/ developmental education to better inform practice. Most work in this area either bemoans poor K–12 preparation or describes programmatic approaches to address so-called under-preparedness. We know that what we are doing is not working, but scholars have not explored important underlying factors. The reason that something so important has been studied to so little good effect has a great deal to do with the hierarchical fallacies discussed in chapter 5.

For example, it would seem that the classic work of Jean Piaget would have helpful applications to remediation. Piaget's (1981) research on cognitive development suggests that students' ability to deal with abstractions—*formal operations* in his term—develops during the teenage years. What could that mean for developmental education in writing and math? Might it be possible to accelerate instruction because of increased cognitive readiness? Research done by Complete College America (CCA, n.d.) would suggest that intensive corequisite remediation works better for many students than more drawn-out remedial work. But why? For whom? For how long?

Cross-disciplinary research is illuminating. How might we apply the findings of neuroscience to learning in general and to remediation in particular? James E. Zull's (2002, 2011) books *The Art of Changing the Brain* and *From Brain to Mind* summarize brain research and possible implications for education at all levels. Zull (2011) highlights the idea that learning is change and "the brain is a natural transformation machine" (p. 16). Applying neuroscience to the remedial/developmental classroom would require leadership, vision, and strategy, and these new ways of thinking might just be transformative.

Another important topic for research is the effect of trauma on student learning. During a report on the retention of under-prepared students at a board of trustees meeting at GSU, a trustee asked what seemed to be a simple question: Are faculty members in social work and psychology studying the effect of trauma on students' ability to learn in foundational courses? We know that we are teaching students who have experienced homelessness, food insecurity, violence, and other traumas. How do we tailor remediation under these circumstances to help traumatized students address academic challenges? GSU's response to this knowledge deficit is to offer small grants to faculty members willing to research such issues. But the educational world needs large-scale investment in cross-disciplinary scholarship conducted by teams of researchers.

So I begin by stipulating that we need much more research. In the rest of this chapter, I describe rethinking and programmatic change based on the little we do know and on common sense. We know that first-generation students are especially vulnerable to dropping out during the first year of college. CCA presents evidence that a significant number of students who begin their college careers with two to four semesters of required, noncredit remedial courses never make it to the first for-credit gateway course. This situation is particularly discouraging for students who test on the cusp of moving into introductory for-credit courses. Many colleges are studying better ways to serve these students.

At GSU, we have been influenced by CCA on corequisite remediation, infusing additional support into the first-year experience, rather than requiring that students take noncredit classes before enrolling in real courses. We designate students as direct admits if they have grade point averages and ACT/SAT scores in the college-ready range. Students who fall somewhat below those criteria (ACT score of 18 and acceptable grades, 2.75 GPA) and who demonstrate motivation and grit are admitted conditionally. GSU is not, however, an open admissions institution. We are willing to do everything possible to accelerate preparation for college success, but we realize that some students may need more time and attention than we can provide. Our recruiters advise students with scores and grades indicating deep problems to enroll in partner community colleges, so they can spend additional time on remediation.

CCA's excellent work has convinced GSU and other universities that corequisite remediation is what they call a "game-changer" for students falling somewhat below conventional criteria. CCA's research is less helpful on what can be done for students who have graduated from high school but are performing at an eighth-grade level or below, especially in writing and reading. Even as we experiment with new approaches, we must take seriously the reservations of experienced educators who are concerned that one CCA size does not fit all.

Remediation in math may be a different story. Typically, assessments of attainment of math skills focus on college algebra, when other capacities in numeracy may be a more relevant indicator for success in college and in many careers. But I would emphasize again the need for comprehensive research on remediation for students who fall significantly below criteria. At GSU, we may have developed game-changers for students on the verge of success. But we must admit that we have not come up with approaches for students with deeper developmental needs. Instead, we send them elsewhere, and they may wind up going nowhere. More research is necessary.

Much of what we do in developmental education is based on common sense and experience. Faculty members are committed to meeting students where they are. That sounds like a simple mantra, but it is actually highly complex. How do we gain knowledge of where students are so that we can meet them there? The first step depends on educating our own imaginations. In his novel *Hard Times*, Charles Dickens (1854) warned nineteenth-century educators not to view students as empty vessels, waiting to be filled with facts. Yet, teachers, especially in developmental courses, may unconsciously adhere to this false metaphor. Or, even worse, imagine that the students' heads are filled with all the wrong things—junk that must be expurgated.

At GSU we use a strength-based model of instruction. During the first week of Smart Start, GSU's fun boot camp in writing and math, I was deeply gratified when I visited a writing class and asked students how things were going. Several hands went up (in itself a happy surprise). The student I called on said, with a degree of enthusiasm not frequently exhibited by students required to end their summer early for two intensive weeks of developmental work, "This class is great because my professor is showing me that I know things." And that's the essence of meeting students where they are and of the strength-based model.

From Smart Start through first-year writing and beyond, students are actually writing; revising; rewriting; editing; and, most important, reading and rereading what they have written. Critical reading of one's own early drafts is one of the skills that is truly basic to learning to write. Our instructors are intentional about teaching this fundamental practice. By doing so, they tacitly take the following pledge: Never allow yourself to be the first human being on the planet to read another person's writing. Make sure that, for starters, the writer has read the material. Techniques of peer review will further protect your psyche from unread prose.

In writing instruction, student and teacher often engage in a tacit contest over responsibility for the text. Students want to get the assignment, for good or ill (usually ill), on the instructor's desk as soon as possible, leading to the submission of unread prose. The instructor, dedicated to student development in writing, too often accepts responsibility as the student's proofreader, editor, or even coauthor. The essence of successful writing instruction is to perfect the role of teacher—one who instills in students responsibility for their own work. Doing so is a challenging task. It's human nature to want to be done with a difficult project. I recall my own experience in writing a chapter for publication in a book edited by a superb editor. He kept sending the chapter back to me, always with excellent suggestions for revision. Finally, I said to him outright that I no longer wanted the chapter to be better. I simply wanted it to be done. If an experienced and confident writer can react in that childish way, how much more patience must we have with novice writers who simply want to be done?

At GSU we provide incentives for extensive reading and revision of students' first writing assignment—a literacy autobiography. Students are asked to write profiles of themselves as writers and readers. This assignment is an excellent way for instructors to know where students are so that they can meet them there. The assignment also encourages reflection on the initial narration. Students revise the essay throughout the academic year and, in the second semester, can submit final versions for monetary awards. My husband and

I personally fund these awards because we believe so much in the process. From a presidential perspective, I also regard this funding as a microphone to communicate the importance of first-year writing and of projects that span more than one semester. Gallup research shows that students benefit enormously from multisemester assignments (Gallup, 2015). The heavily revised literacy autobiography gives form to the concept of meeting students where they are and challenging them to move forward.

Learning to write by writing is a commonsense principle that must be applied to developmental and gateway courses. Unfortunately, too many remedial courses focus on correcting grammatical errors. When students go public with writing, they must, no doubt, demonstrate control over sentence structure, grammar, usage, punctuation, and spelling. These surface features are what readers see first and can lead to rejection of the writing and the writer. I tell students that the worst thing that an instructor can do is to give the student a low grade. In the world outside the university, something much more damaging happens. The reader stops reading and hits the delete key.

Once again common sense dictates that writers will never be motivated to correct surface features unless they are first committed to what they are writing—communicating their ideas to achieve personal goals. Can you imagine what would happen if we taught baseball the way some teach writing? In this ineffective remedial baseball scenario, coaches would sit players down and force them to memorize everything that could go wrong on the field. Learners would not be permitted to play until they passed tests on the rules. Although the motivation might be to avoid injury, the result would be disaster. I would argue that much remedial writing instruction results in the equivalent of writer's block. In baseball, as in writing, learning can and should take place in real

To build empathy for the novice, I have the following recommendation for all instructors: Periodically, try to do something that you have no natural aptitude for. For me that activity was always easy to find because I have no propensity for anything athletic, even though I have always tried extremely hard to accomplish assignments, athletic or otherwise. My eighth-grade gym instructor required what looked to me to be contortions on the rings, ropes, and stall bars. I tried and tried, even arriving at school to practice in the early morning hours before my regular class schedule, but to no avail. Despite this hard work, the gym instructor gave me a D, keeping me off the distinguished honor roll—something that still stings decades later.

But even this form of borderline psychological child abuse did not deter me from trying to participate in sports. As an adult teaching college composition, I tried to learn to ski. My friends skied frequently in Killington, Vermont, and I wanted to be in the party. I opted for private lessons with Sven, Killington's expert ski instructor. I realized that I had to tell him up front that he would have to show me how to do things that he never thought he would have to explain to a functioning adult. He was not a good teacher. But his sneering attitude taught me an important lesson about my own teaching of composition: Don't judge students who have to struggle to learn what comes easily to you. Frequent lessons in humility and empathy would, I believe, improve remedial/developmental education, as well as ski instruction.

Another commonsense element in successful remediation is to avoid making students feel stupid—and that doesn't involve coddling them. Instructors are proud of their own fluency and may be tempted to model their expertise to impress students. I recall the classic story about the nineteenth-century woman who met with the two great British prime ministers, Gladstone and Disraeli. She commented that her meeting with Gladstone led her to believe that she had just met the smartest person on earth. Her meeting with Disraeli, however, made her think that she herself was an intelligent and interesting person. Students learn more from Disraeli-like instructors than they do from the Gladstone type. Human beings remember how another person makes them feel. We remember much less about what they tell us to do.

Focusing on students' strengths does not involve spoon-feeding, condescension, or false praise for trivial accomplishments. It's a great deal more difficult to identify and articulate what someone is doing right than to point out what is going wrong. Another sports analogy is when Joe Maddon, the Chicago Cubs' manager, was quoted in the *Chicago Tribune* saying the following about Jason Heyward, one of his players: "There are all these different moments that occur that we don't recognize because we see only the obvious. He's not hitting

.300, so obviously people think he's not playing well, which is so far from the truth. He makes a great impact by his presence." Maddon talks about Heyward's "butterfly effect," motivating his teammates to perform at the top of their talent, and Heyward's own ability to get on base and play high-quality defense (Gonzales, 2016). Just so, instructors in developmental courses, and really in all courses, must exercise a high level of analysis to identify and motivate students to build on their strengths.

Many of these commonsense principles are at the heart of outstanding research done by Shaun Harper (2014) and also by Gallup (2015). Harper focuses his research on Black males who suffer especially from the deficit model. From 1997 to 2012 Harper studied programs designed specifically to improve the college performance of Black males and found vast differences between "intended" and "actual" effects. Harper argues that the "near exclusive focus on problems . . . inadvertently reinforced a hopeless, deficit-oriented narrative" (p. 127). He calls for detailed studies of the one-third of Black men who did complete college rather than dwelling on the two-thirds who did not.

Here is another opportunity for research. We need more studies focused on students who succeed, especially when they have done so in the face of institutional and systemic obstacles. Shaun Harper and John Kuykendall (2012), focusing on success initiatives for Black males, call for meaningfully engaging Black undergraduate men "as collaborators and . . . experts in designing, implementing, and assessing campus initiatives" (p. 25). Research partnership between faculty and undergraduate scholars might be a start in creating the knowledge we need not only to design programs but also to understand what makes these programs succeed—or not.

The most important point in Harper's research is that "fixing the student" does not work. Instead we must look at transforming universities so that students will have a better chance of succeeding. Fundamental to that transformation is a commitment to analyzing student strengths rather than focusing on deficits. In a speech, "It's the Educonomy, Stupid," delivered on June 30, 2014, to the Education Commission of the States and broadcast on CNN, Brandon Busteed, Gallup's executive director of education and workforce development, urged replacing a deficit-based lens with a strength-based lens. Like Shaun Harper, Busteed rejects remediation. The underlying premise of the Gallup research is the effectiveness and long-term impact of building on what is right about students rather than fixing what is wrong. Busteed points to the "amazing impact of teachers who make students excited about the future." He highlights these major factors leading to student success: "working on long-term projects, applying learning to the community, knowing that teachers care about them." These attributes coincide with AAC&U's high-impact practices (Kuh, 2008).

Extensive research by Gallup demonstrates that the strength model is effective at institutions of all types for all students, from those in developmental courses to those in honors sections. The 2014 Gallup-Purdue Index report *Great Jobs, Great Lives* studies more than 30,000 college graduates across the United States. One indicator of success is college completion, so studying college graduates is a starting point in discovering the strengths that led them to succeed. It's important to note that Gallup and Purdue avoided simplistic and misleading measures of success, such as salaries for first jobs. Instead, they "created an index that examines long-term success of graduates as they pursue a good job and a better life" (Gallup, 2014, p. 3). *Great Jobs, Great Lives* elaborates as follows:

> For example, if graduates had a professor who cared about them as a person, made them excited about learning, and encouraged them to pursue their dreams, their odds of being engaged at work more than doubled, as did their odds of thriving in their well-being. And if graduates had an internship or job where they were able to apply what they were learning in the classroom, were actively involved in extracurricular activities and organizations, and worked on projects that took a semester or more to complete, their odds of being engaged at work doubled also. Feeling supported and having deep learning experiences means everything. (p. 6)

Gallup (2014) invites "a national dialogue on improving the college experience" (p. 19), with instructors making assignments that build on students' strengths and encourage real-life applications of classroom learning.

Attention to real-life applications of classroom learning applies directly to reform in developmental math. Uri Treisman, professor of mathematics and public affairs and director of the Charles A. Dana Center at the University of Texas at Austin, calls for a revolution in redesigning math pathways. CCA endorses what Treisman calls "the stat way to heaven" as a major game-changer in college completion. Gearing math requirements to students' general career directions, called *meta-majors* by CCA, would remove significant barriers to student success, while providing rigorous preparation in mathematical thinking that is actually relevant to students' future achievements. Treisman is a charter member, along with William E. Kirwan, former chancellor of the University System of Maryland, of Transforming Post-Secondary Education in Mathematics (TPSE Math), funded by the Carnegie Corporation of New York and the Alfred P. Sloan Foundation. Major mathematical organizations like the Mathematical Association of America support TPSE Math's goals (Logue, 2016).

Research conducted at CUNY and reported in the American Educational Research Association's *Educational Evaluation and Policy Analysis* journal demonstrates significantly higher success rates for remedial students following a statistics pathway rather than those assigned to the traditional route to calculus through intermediate algebra. For example, 56% passed college-level statistics, whereas only 39% passed elementary algebra (as cited in Smith, 2016). Reform in math pathways should begin in high school. Across the country, 11th-graders who don't do well in intermediate algebra are told that they are not college material. If we put aside the exercising-the-brain-cells argument—an exercise that can just as well be achieved in courses in statistics or mathematical reasoning—the only purpose for intermediate algebra is to prepare students to take calculus. Although we certainly want to encourage and support students who wish to go into STEM fields, science, technology, engineering, and theoretical mathematics are not the only pathways to success. Many high-stakes math tests focus on concepts in intermediate algebra, creating insurmountable barriers for students who might be on track for success in the majority of leadership careers that require statistics rather than algebra. Reform is essential.

Many states, including Illinois, that endorse core courses for transfer to any college or university already build in a choice between the calculus pathway and the statistics pathway. At GSU, freshmen indicate meta-majors. Do they wish to prepare for study in STEM, or are they instead exploring the social sciences, humanities, arts, education, health professions, or business? Accordingly, students in two of three freshman learning communities take statistics, and those in the other freshman learning community take precalculus. It's interesting to note that a number of scientific fields do not require calculus. We can advise students accordingly and send them on the stat-way to heaven—or at least on the road to a leadership career.

Figuring out the appropriate math requirement for students is another instance of teaching to students' strengths rather than to their deficits. From the beginning of their GSU experience, students become part of a community focused on what is right with them rather than what is wrong. The Smart Start two-week summer program, in addition to courses in writing and/or in math, requires students to begin Mastering College, a one-credit course that continues through the first semester. Mastering College, coordinated by a psychology professor, guides each student through the Clifton StrengthsFinder and uses StrengthsQuest (Clifton & Anderson, 2004) as a program guide. Direct admits, students who are not required to take Smart Start, are advised that the StrengthsFinder is available to them in Career Services. Freshman Seminar, a three-credit interdisciplinary humanities course required of all students, highlights the role of personal strengths in the systems analyses at the seminar's intellectual core.

All freshmen benefit from teams of advisers and counselors assigned to each learning community. The idea is to integrate support into every student's experience rather than sending so-called deficient students to special treatment centers to cure their difficulties. Peer mentors, cohort advisers, career specialists, writing consultants, library liaisons, digital learning experts, psychological counselors, and faculty from the CJY are assigned to each freshman/sophomore cohort. For students living in student housing—Prairie Place—three faculty-in-residence are available at the odd hours appropriate to a living-learning community. The clear message is that asking for help is not a display of weakness, exposing students' deficits, but instead a mature approach to learning and growing. Active engagement with the support teams builds on students' strengths.

The Academic Cohort Honoring Efficacy and Valuing Education (ACHIEVE) program is open to all freshmen but mandatory for students requiring special support. This *corequisite remediation*, as CCA terms it, offers tutoring sessions for English and math, including MyStatsLab. Faculty members track student progress by monitoring attendance, attitude, and participation. Midterm grades provide an early warning system.

These academic measures are complemented by a full-scale, intentional commitment in student life to the strengths-based model. Talking circles and leadership seminars are available to the student body in general and also to segmented groups, respecting the idea that in some instances women, men, people of color, and members of the LGBTQ community may find it easier to discover and capitalize on their strengths in confidential, protected conversations. *Capitalization* is the concept of moving from identifying strengths to applying them enthusiastically to a variety of circumstances (Bowers & Lopez, 2010). We need much more research on capitalization.

I began this chapter with an appeal for more research on remedial/developmental education, and so I conclude. Responding to what seem on the surface to be straightforward suggestions actually requires cultural transformations in the academy. We must explore and expunge several unexamined assumptions. Teaching to strengths is not condescending or patronizing. It's difficult. It's revolutionary. Barriers to its application are connected to stereotyping. Where are the scholars ready to study, uncover, and reform entrenched attitudes and practices? Real and necessary change is impeded by vested interests and false hierarchies (see chapter 5). We have the vision. We can formulate the strategy. We can do the research. But first we need the courage to rethink and transform remediation.

7

SEAMLESS PATHWAYS FROM THE COMMUNITY COLLEGES TO UNIVERSITY GRADUATION

This chapter posits that twenty-first-century universities must develop intentional, high-quality pathways from the community colleges to university graduation. That task should not be left entirely to the community colleges. Two-year college experts like Pamela L. Eddy (2010) recognize that "community colleges have become the nexus of educational partnerships forming what policy makers envision as seamless educational pathways from kindergarten through baccalaureate" (p. 3). But the community colleges cannot be expected to create these pathways alone. University leaders must accept responsibility and work in active partnership with community college colleagues.

Here, I describe and draw on the success of GSU's DDP—our award-winning partnership with 17 Chicago-area community colleges—to illustrate a scalable model for enhanced university/community college cooperation and reference other types of community college/university partnerships that I have personally overseen. The idea is to be student centered, to recognize that some students are better served by a four-year undergraduate program offered on a university campus, whereas others will thrive with a coherent four-year pathway starting in the community college or even earlier in the high school with a 2+2+2 program. Both/and, not either/or, should be the rule.

Throughout my career I have been committed to making connections and breaking down barriers. WAC is an example of horizontal connections; cooperation with K–12 schools and community colleges works vertically. Silos within the university are difficult to transcend because of disciplinary commitments and the lack of doctoral preparation in university citizenship. Vertical partnerships are even more challenging because of the hierarchical fallacy discussed in chapter 5. It's difficult for university faculty members to see their community college counterparts as colleagues. And this inherent lack of respect pertains even more emphatically to K–12 teachers. Initiatives like the NWP that bring together teachers from various levels of instruction have achieved unquestioned success in mapping coherent learning plans for students. But the overall educational culture promotes separation.

Recognizing these hierarchical divides is the first step in overcoming them. University leaders are well advised to organize seminars, workshops, and symposia that bring together university instructors with faculty members from feeder community colleges. These seminars should be organized around intellectual topics and should not be an occasion for the university faculty to lecture—profess to—colleagues from the community colleges. In fact, community college professors can bring much-needed expertise on a wide range of topics, including that great unknown: understanding the first-generation college student.

Creating a healthy context for these grassroots connections depends on respectful colleagueship between university and community college presidents. In the spring of 1996, when it was initially announced that I would be the next head of ASU West, the first person to congratulate me was Tessa Martinez-Pollack, then the president of Glendale Community College (GCC), the campus within the Maricopa Community College system that was geographically closest to ASU West. Even before I set foot in Arizona, Martinez-Pollack and I were corresponding about partnerships between our two institutions. My first initiative as campus CEO was to work with Martinez-Pollack on a memorandum of understanding (MOU) establishing what we called the University/College Center.

In effect, we arranged for GCC to establish a small campus at ASU West. University/college students signed up for a zero-credit, zero-cost ASU course, which gave them access to the entire ASU library system. University/college students could join both GCC and ASU West student clubs. They paid tuition to GCC, and they were taught mostly by GCC faculty members, but they were welcome participants in the life of a university campus. Only full-time GCC faculty members were invited to teach at ASU West, and the university provided office space and, even more important, opportunities for community college colleagues to interact as peers with university faculty members.

At the beginning of the project, ASU West was an upper-division campus. GCC University/College Center faculty members were invited to participate in an exchange in which they taught some junior and senior ASU West courses. Carefully selected ASU West faculty members taught GCC freshman and sophomore courses. These interactions went far in establishing colleagueship between community college and university faculty members and in breaking down the hierarchical fallacy. ASU West charged no rent for this small GCC campus on university property. So what did ASU West get out of the arrangement? The university created a culture of cooperation and helped community college students to think about a four-year pathway, with many of them eventually transferring to ASU West.

In addition to providing excellent opportunities for students, this cooperative program built trust between the university and all Maricopa Community Colleges. It soon became clear that the colocation of a community college and university served some students but not all. Even with the University/College Center option, hundreds of students continued to fill ASU buses departing from the West campus to attend freshman and sophomore classes 40 miles away at ASU's main campus in Tempe. When we formally surveyed the students on the buses, we found that a vast majority stated a preference for a four-year university experience on the ASU West campus.

In August 2001, ASU West admitted its first freshman class. The University/College Center was the major reason that the Phoenix-area community colleges did not oppose ASU West becoming a four-year university. By putting students first through a colocation model, we built trust with the community colleges. We promised that we would continue the University/College Center after we admitted our first freshmen. And we did. In fact, as we reviewed applications for direct admission to ASU West, we invited students who did not meet ASU West admissions criteria to be part of our university campus community through the University/College Center. In that way students were encouraged to start at a community college but have access to a university. Instead of saying, "No," we could say, "Not yet." ASU West sustained the colocation with GCC for a few years after I departed from the university in 2004. Other changes in ASU's administrative structure led to different ways of cooperating with the Maricopa Community Colleges.

The sustainability of community college/university pathways is a challenge. It is essential to create infrastructure, policies, and funding sources that transcend particular administrations. The initiative originally known in the mid-1980s as the Vassar/LaGuardia project still exists 30 years later under the title Exploring Transfer (ET), but in a form quite different from its origins. Originally, the idea was for Vassar to partner with a single community college to provide pathways for transfer and, by doing so, create a scalable model for other community college partnerships with four-year colleges and universities. Funding from the Ford Foundation and other sources encouraged these partnerships. In the 1990s, for example, Arcadia University (formerly Beaver College) developed a program with the Community College of Philadelphia, as did community colleges and universities in other regions across the nation, but these partnerships did not last.

Today, ET selects first-generation, high-achieving community college students from a list of about 15 community colleges, including LaGuardia, to attend summer courses cotaught by Vassar and community college professors. These 15 community colleges employ ET coordinators to assist in recruiting honors students for this all-expenses-paid opportunity. Community college students may be pursuing associate degrees in either traditional transfer or career technical programs. During the summer they are introduced to intensive study of the liberal arts. The ET website reports that during its 30 years of existence, more than 1,000 students have participated, with over 80% transferring to 4-year institutions.

The ET program is exemplary in a number of ways. It recognizes the need for community college students to have a strong background in the liberal arts. Vassar professors and community college professors teach together in the program and thereby break down the hierarchical fallacy. Students have opportunities to expand their horizons and to aspire to educational attainment that will take them well beyond narrow preparation for a first job. I hope that ET thrives and expands, but it is a diminished version of the numerous university/community college partnerships launched in the 1990s. Because of lack of funding, changes in administration, and other reasons, the scalability of the original Vassar/LaGuardia project has been lost.

As chancellor of UAA, I encountered another model for community college/university partnership. Alaska supports three state universities—UAA, University of Alaska Fairbanks, and University of Alaska Southeast—all under a single University of Alaska board of regents and a president of the system. Each of the three universities, under the leadership of a chancellor, oversees the community colleges in the appropriate geographic area. I had responsibility for community colleges in the Kenai Peninsula, Kachemak Bay, Valdez, and Kodiak Island. In addition, UAA housed a two-year college on its main campus in Anchorage. Particularly on the Anchorage campus but to varying degrees with the more far-flung community colleges, the pathways to the bachelor's degree were mapped out well for students. The model itself may lack scalability, however. In those places that already have similar built-in administrative connections between community colleges and universities, I would advise taking advantage of the existing structures for full integration and intentionality. Creating such structures where they do not already exist would be needlessly disruptive—and not in a good sense. It's much more important to create disruption in breaking down hierarchical fallacies than in compromising the existing autonomy of community colleges and universities. The less bureaucracy, the better. Partnership is better than dismantling autonomous administrative structures.

When I arrived at GSU on July 1, 2007, I had a list of those whom I should call on the first day of my presidency that included the presidents of the community colleges geographically closest to our location in south suburban Chicago. In my installation speech on November 3, 2007, I articulated the vision for university/community college cooperation as follows:

My goal is to learn how GSU can improve the record of baccalaureate completion for students who begin their college careers
at community colleges. Each community college, true to its
unique location and mission, has excellent suggestions for working together. I envision a Community College Compact. GSU
will continue to listen and learn from our community college colleagues. We intend to share facilities and faculty, to recruit jointly
at high schools, and to coordinate advising. Our shared goal is to
increase the number of community college transfers attaining a
bachelor's degree, and beyond. (Maimon, 2007)

My vision included providing debt-free baccalaureate education
for low-income community college transfer students. Then, as now,
the vast majority of minority students begin their college careers at
community colleges. In 2007, the completion rates were depressing—
only 16% graduating within 6 years (National Student Clearinghouse
Research Center, 2016a), and these national percentages have not
changed much since. Fear of debt is a major obstacle to motivating
economically struggling, first-generation college students to complete
college. When we say "financial aid," many students hear "loans,"
even though outright grants are available. Then, as now, many do not
complete the FAFSA. Instead, they take on additional jobs and sign
up for fewer courses. Often the extra income decreases their eligibility
for grants, and the lower course load makes them less likely to finish
their degrees—ever.

The first fund-raising campaign initiated under my presidency
was the GSU Promise, designed to establish an endowment to sup-
plement federal and state funds for students transferring to GSU
from Chicagoland community colleges. My husband and I immediately donated an initial $10,000 to this endowment in honor
of my presidential predecessor, Stuart Fagan. In June 2016, GSU
completed the initial goal of raising $1 million—the largest single
endowment for our young university.

Community college leaders were favorably impressed that we
put our money where our mouth was in supporting community
college transfer students. The next step was to meet and listen to
community college colleagues about what would work, or not, in
attempting to increase completion rates. The listening was most
important. I must confess that my first instinct was to suggest the

colocation model to the president and provost of the community college geographically closest to us, Prairie State College (PSC). This model had served students and won awards in Arizona. Why not in Illinois? It took me a while—probably too long—to understand that, for various reasons, the Arizona approach was not going to be successful in the south suburbs of Chicago. Rent-free space was not an incentive for PSC, as it had been in Phoenix. Also, I had to change perspectives to understand that colocation worked in Arizona in part because the president of GCC had herself suggested it and therefore had full ownership of the plan. Something imported from another state by a new university president was undoubtedly going to be met with some suspicion.

In fact, I began to hear about incidents in GSU's history of relationships with community colleges, especially nearby PSC. Four presidents before me had begun their terms of office with high hopes for enhanced community college cooperation, but these well-meaning beginnings did not result in improved interactions. According to Linda Uzureau, the PSC provost, GSU did not listen sufficiently to community college advice and did not develop strategies for cooperation up and down the ranks to instill real change. After a few missteps, I began to hear what the community college leaders were saying about the conditions for breaking down hierarchies and establishing game-changing cooperation.

After my two-and-a-half year community college listening tour, on April 30, 2010, GSU convened a summit to initiate the Chicagoland Alliance for Degree Completion, attended by administration and faculty from several community colleges, including the five geographically closest to the university: PSC, South Suburban College, Moraine Valley Community College, Kankakee Community College, and Joliet Junior College. Later the alliance would include the seven campuses of the City Colleges of Chicago and five additional community colleges at further distances in the Chicagoland area.

GSU and six community colleges signed the original Statement of Principles and Commitment. Because this core document established the foundation for the DDP, it's worth quoting in its entirety (see box 7.1). The formality of the document was necessary to establish lasting changes in the infrastructure of the institutions. The initial alliance summit was public, with a ceremonial feel to it, essential so that deans, faculty members, and counselors from the university

---

BOX 7.1.
The Chicagoland Alliance for Degree Completion Statement of
Principles and Commitment

STATEMENT OF PRINCIPLES AND COMMITMENT
SEPTEMBER 22, 2010

RECOGNIZING that, nationally, more than 40% of high school graduates start their postsecondary education at 2-year institutions; and that, since the beginning of the Great Recession, increasing numbers of students, especially those who are the first in their families to attend college, are beginning their bachelor's degree study at community college;

REALIZING that of the total number of students who begin at community colleges directly from high school, only 10% complete a 4-year degree after 6 years of study and that the comparable rates for African American and Latino students—at 5.9% and 3.1%, respectively—are even more disturbing;

ALARMED by the fact that only 21% of students enrolling at Illinois' community colleges graduate with associate degrees in three years and that comparable degree completion rates for African Americans and Hispanics—at 9% and 13%, respectively—are even more startling;

NOTING WITH DISAPPOINTMENT that the United States, which was once first among nations, now ranks 10th in the proportion of young adults achieving a college degree and that this dismal performance poses a threat to our nation's global competitiveness;

BEING SUPPORTIVE of the national goal set by President Barack Obama to reverse this slippage by ensuring that

> "an additional five million Americans complete degrees and certificates in the next decade" and that the United States will "have the highest proportion of college graduates in the world";

AWARE of projections that, in less than 10 years, more than 60% of all new jobs will require a college degree;

BOX 7.1.

CONCERNED that these trends are increasingly perpetuating economic insecurity and inequality;

RECOGNIZING that the institutions that we lead collectively serve over 170,000 students each and every year—and that the number is growing; and

PAINFULLY AWARE that "access without success is an empty promise,"

WE, THE UNDERSIGNED, have come together on this 22nd day of September, 2010, on the campus of Governors State University, to establish the **Chicagoland Alliance for Degree Completion**, to serve as the organizational vehicle and expression of our commitment, both individual and collective, to accelerate student success toward timely matriculation and degree completion from our institutions. Toward this goal, we will:

1. engage in collaborative programs, efforts and activities that facilitate and enhance student success toward matriculation and degree completion;
2. collaborate to simplify the transfer process for bachelor's degree completion by engaging in such endeavors as curricular articulation, dual admission, establishment and operation of degree completion centers, coordination of admission and financial aid advising, information sharing, etc.;
3. advocate together to promote public awareness and support;
4. work together to assist students in accessing and securing financial aid; and
5. meet regularly to assess our progress toward these goals.

---

and the community college could bear witness. The effectiveness of these actions has stood the test of time. In fact, five of the original seven signatory presidents are no longer at their colleges, but the DDP remains strong.

As we planned the inaugural meeting for the Chicagoland Alliance, I sought help from Linda Uzureau, who had recently retired as provost of PSC. An outspoken skeptic of university overtures, Uzureau always spoke her mind and provided excellent advice. It became clear that I had to do everything in my power to convince Uzureau to put off full retirement and agree to join GSU as an assistant to the president for community college partnerships. With 30 years of experience at 3 south suburban community colleges, Uzureau was also the perfect liaison to build trust with our partners. Community college leaders knew that if Uzureau supported something, it must be real. She would not promote anything superficial, and she would always keep community college interests in the forefront. Uzureau filled this essential partnership role for 6 years, finally opting for full retirement in June 2016. By that time GSU had established a track record worthy of confidence.

An important lesson: Leading academic change is made much easier when a strong critic is a person of goodwill, shares your vision for student success, and is ready to work with you strategically. Uzureau's community college experience and intellectual clarity were essential in developing the principles of the DDP. For those not lucky enough to find someone like Uzureau, the key to transformational change is to listen to people—community college leaders in this instance—who are addressing challenges from very different perspectives.

Inspired by the April 2010 summit, we continued work on what was to become the DDP partnership with 17 community colleges. We call the program *dual degree* (very different from dual enrollment agreements between colleges and high schools) because a fundamental principle of DDP is encouragement by the university for community college students to complete their associate degrees *at the community college*. I openly admit that in my career-long commitment to community college/university partnerships, it had never before occurred to me what should have been obvious: We at the university should be encouraging students to complete the associate degree before transferring. Even those opposed to hierarchies can be afflicted by systemic hierarchical thinking. I must confess that at ASU West, with a full commitment to the University/College Center, I assumed without careful analysis or reference to research findings that students would be best served by becoming full-fledged university students as soon as possible.

In Illinois, I learned from my community college colleagues, especially from Linda Uzureau, that the research is irrefutable.

Students who complete community college associate degrees are much more likely to complete university bachelor's degrees when they transfer. The reasons are clear. Finishing one degree builds confidence for completing a second degree. We know that students are prone to drop out because of a crisis in confidence. In addition, a degree—as opposed to a smorgasbord of random courses, sometimes at multiple institutions—has intellectual coherence, providing students with a solid base to build on (Doyle, 2006; Rosenbaum, Diel-Amen, & Person, 2006). I bring the zeal of a recent convert to this concept.

In our DDP agreements and in university policy, GSU affirms that the university will not recruit students at partner community colleges—any students, not just those enrolled in the DDP—until they are on track to complete the community college associate degree. In addition, GSU requires that DDP students be enrolled in 15 credits per semester—"15 to Finish," in CCA's phrase. Through the DDP, we join community college counselors in advising students that full-time study does not preclude holding a job. In fact, 15 to Finish creates coherence in students' course work and a greater likelihood of completing the associate degree and then the bachelor's degree (Complete College America, n.d.). Full-time study through the DDP is also more economical, opening up possibilities for federal and state grants, as well as other scholarship support, keeping students on track to complete requirements and to take prerequisite courses.

With these two principles—encouragement from the university for students to complete community college degrees and to do so through full-time study—we found the Holy Grail in community college/university relationships: The university must take an active role in supporting these principles, which benefit students and can be adopted anywhere. In other words, they are fully scalable. The principles also promote additional student credit hours (SCHs) at the community colleges. Given the basis for most community college funding formulas, university support for more SCHs there builds trust. Together we are not arguing over a too-small pie. We are working to help more students complete two degrees—the associate and then the bachelor's, creating a bigger pie—always in the interest of students.

It is also important for the university to invest in students while they are still attending the community college. GSU provides transfer specialists (not recruiters) who spend four days per week working with community college counselors to advise students on site at the community colleges. The DDP is emphatically student centered. From the start, we have emphasized that our goal is to help students complete high-quality bachelor's degrees at whatever university is best suited to their needs. GSU willingly borrows a strategy from the great holiday movie *Miracle on Thirty-Fourth Street.* Kris Kringle, as the Macy's department store Santa, would send families to Gimbel's if Macy's did not have a particular desired toy. Macy's did not lose with that family-centered practice. Just so, GSU does not lose by centering on students' needs and desires for degree completion.

For those students who select GSU, we provide scholarships through the GSU Promise Endowment. These scholarships are over and above federal and state grants. Our goal is for DDP students to graduate without debt—or with as little debt as possible. Financial aid counselors advise students on scholarship opportunities and financial management. Enhanced counseling and advising help DDP students complete the associate degree in five semesters, with the first semester devoted to the completion of remedial work, if necessary.

As DDP students transfer to GSU, we select the best prepared and most enthusiastic to be peer mentors, who visit their community college alma maters to work with new students entering the pipeline. In addition, peer mentors are available to help DDP transfers in their first GSU semester. DDP students have access to the services of the CJY (described in chapter 8) and join GSU students for plays, pizza parties, and other on-campus events.

Ceremonies are important. We hold an induction ceremony at GSU for new entrants into the DDP. Students receive cords in the school colors of their community colleges. Before their GSU graduation, these community college colors are braided with GSU's base colors of black and white, signifying the cooperation of the community college and the university in students' success. These braided cords are presented at a special ceremony during graduation week, and the DDP students wear the cords proudly during commencement. Community college presidents are invited to sit on the GSU commencement stage to share in the celebration of students' accomplishments through two institutions of higher education. In addition, at graduation time GSU sends community college presidents lists of all graduates (not just DDP participants) who started at their colleges. It's important for the university to affirm to the community colleges that we did this together.

For students one of the most important features of the DDP is the motivation from the beginning of their higher education careers to think ahead to four years, not just two. For most students a two-year degree is not enough to prepare for life in the twenty-first century. Politicians and the media have created confusion on this point. Two-year career/technical degrees may be a beginning—or an addition—to four-year degrees. But research shows that bachelor's degrees not only prepare students for lifelong higher incomes (Carnevale, Rose, & Cheah, 2011) but also make it more likely that graduates will be healthier (Egerter, Braveman, Sadegh-Nobari, Grossman-Kahn, & Dekker, 2009), happier, and more civically engaged (Pew Research Center, 2013).

The DDP's emphasis on four-year thinking can prevent unnecessary detours. For example, physical therapists require a doctorate for licensure. Yet, many first-generation students, eager to study something that sounds like a job, may follow a career/technical path in a physical therapy assistant (PTA) program. GSU is one of a handful of universities offering degree completion for students in all career/technical programs through limited pathways, providing liberal arts/general education at the upper division to match the specialization at the lower division. Thus, DDP students with community college PTA training would be able to complete a bachelor's degree in four-and-a-half years. While the PTA alone provides limited opportunities for advancement, the experience of hands-on work with patients could provide a basis for excelling in a bachelor's completion degree and then going on to doctoral level study. But those aspiring to become physical therapists might be better advised to pursue a liberal arts associate degree at the community college and then build on that at a university like GSU, which offers the doctorate in physical therapy (DPT). Physical therapy faculty members can advise students on preparatory undergraduate courses and on the high performance standards necessary for attaining professional credentials.

The more we work with DDP students, the more we understand how complicated it is for first-generation college students to find clear pathways to success. One student said in a focus group,

"Before I discovered the DDP, I was on a dark and winding road without a flashlight." The DDP is the flashlight, illuminating pathways for students. Nationally, it's important to recognize that these pathways can seem like a maze to the uninitiated. Let's be clear on what we are asking students to do. Without programs like the DDP, we are challenging novices, most without a higher education support network, to find their way through not one bureaucracy but two. The least we can do as leaders of these daunting bureaucracies is to talk with each other and illuminate the roadway.

GSU appreciates the support of the Kresge Foundation, which on November 29, 2012, awarded GSU a grant to build on the initial momentum of the DDP. With Kresge support, we have increased the number of partner community colleges from 5 to 17, with robust enrollments from the City Colleges of Chicago (CCC). GSU was 1 of the first 2 universities willing to partner with CCC on the STAR scholarship program, targeting high-achieving Chicago public school students, who enter full-time, 2-year degree programs at CCC at no cost. GSU offers special scholarships to STAR students once they come to GSU through the DDP.

In addition, Kresge has provided initial funding for an online 12-credit-hour graduate certificate of advanced study in student success and completion, available nationally to community college and university faculty and staff. The certificate has been integrated into a new track in GSU's master of arts in counseling, with the goal of helping counselors, advisers, and mentors assist community college students in bachelor's degree completion. GSU also offers forums for in-service counselors and for students and community members who are interested in exploring careers in student development. Our goal is to help advisers become better informed about unconventional completion pathways like the DDP.

In 2015, at the conclusion of GSU's first grant from the Kresge Foundation, we absorbed the full costs for transfer specialists, peer mentors, and other employees who had been partially supported on the grant. Giving priority to the DDP, we integrated these expenditures in our base budget, even during challenging fiscal times in Illinois. Kresge gave us permission to use remaining grant funds to launch the male success initiative (MSI), supporting male students of color, most of whom begin in community colleges but never complete either associate or bachelor's degrees. A new Kresge grant, awarded in the fall of 2016, allows GSU to expand and deepen the MSI; develop 2+2+2 pathways from the junior year in high school to the community college to GSU; and disseminate the DDP nationally through web materials, campus seminars, and conferences.

GSU has fulfilled the initial vision of creating navigable pathways from 17 Chicagoland community colleges to university graduation. In its first 6 years, an average of 91% of DDP students who transfer to GSU have either graduated or are on track to graduate. The GSU board of trustees has mandated as a presidential goal that the university maintain or exceed that graduation rate.

DDP students are diverse; 46% are students of color. There is no achievement gap between DDP transfer students of color and other students. In fact, DDP students have been elected as student trustees and as Lincoln Laureates (the highest honor awarded to one student each year at each Illinois university). A sizeable number of DDP students go on to pursue graduate and professional degrees at GSU and elsewhere.

In addition to students who move directly from high school to the community college, a surprising number of returning adults have found success in the DDP. Some testify that the coherence of the program and the structured collegiality have made it possible for them to take 15 to Finish each semester—and actually to finish. One such student won a generous fellowship to attend law school full-time. Nonetheless, we realize that students with families and mortgages may require different approaches, including part-time attendance. GSU's original emphasis was on helping students—no matter their age—to finish what they start. With the help of the Lumina Foundation, we are part of a five-university consortium to do just that. Many students applying through the consortium have community college credits from a variety of institutions. As universities develop closer and more respectful relationships with community colleges, they will be better prepared to recognize and suitably package credits acquired there.

In these perplexing financial times, some community colleges are offering or proposing to offer bachelor's degrees. Such aspirations drive a wedge between community colleges and universities, leading to unnecessary turf battles. Community colleges have a special mission to provide high-quality associate degrees. Lack of appropriate respect from universities and the general public for foundational work leads to community colleges seeking what some consider a more elevated place in the hierarchy. Higher education is not well served by additional four-year public colleges, when most states can't support the bachelor's-degree-granting institutions that they already have. Partnership, like the DDP, is the answer, serving students and the public interest.

The community colleges under the auspices of CUNY have established exemplary guided pathways from their honors programs to honors programs at New York City's 4-year public universities. In 2011, for the first time in 40 years, CUNY established a new community college, Guttman Community College, structured on research-based principles. Guttman offers "an integrated first-year curriculum that is inquiry-based and majors that prepare students for baccalaureate study" (Guttman Community College, n.d.). CUNY's 4-year colleges work closely with Guttman to provide seamless transfer.

In a rural environment that could not be more different from New York City, the University of Texas Rio Grande Valley, founded in 2013, works with partner community colleges and K–12 institutions to offer 2+2+2 and 2+4 programs to students. Nate Simpson, a program officer at the Bill & Melinda Gates Foundation, told me about this most promising partnership in Texas (personal communication, June 8, 2017).

The AACC, with support from the Bill & Melinda Gates Foundation, and other funding sources, has created The Pathways Project, establishing and expanding course and career pathways at 30 community colleges in 17 states (Smith, 2016). These pathways are for the most part self-contained within the community colleges. Although clear guidance to associate degree completion is necessary, universities should be cooperating with local community colleges to create bridges, like the DDP, to university graduation.

Texas A&M University College Station (Texas A&M), for example, has partnered with Dallas' Richland College and El Centro College to establish the Chevron Engineering Academy. This partnership between the four-year flagship university and the community colleges establishes coenrollment for selected students in a seamless pathway to a university degree. This project focuses on educating a new generation of engineers who can get their start at low-tuition, but high-quality, community colleges. The Chevron

Engineering Academy has a limited focus, but it is a step in the right direction (Morris, 2017). I hope that Texas A&M and other Dallas area universities will continue to work with El Centro and Richland on DDP-type programs. The DDP is entirely scalable, because it is based on the following simple principles: respect for the coherence and quality of community college programs, encouragement from the university to complete the associate degree at the community college, university investment in joint advising of community college students while they are still on the community college campus, and both the community college and the university providing incentives for full-time enrollment (15 to Finish). Beginning in the summer of 2018, GSU will offer Kresge-supported institutes for university/community college teams to plan cooperative programs for students in their geographic regions.

As the twenty-first century proceeds, these university/community college partnerships become more and more imperative, if the nation is to achieve broad-based student success. I call on presidents of universities to lead academic change by actively putting some skin in the game and not waiting passively for community college students to show up. I call on presidents of community colleges to overcome distrust—justifiable as it may be, given the hierarchical fallacy—and work with neighboring universities to provide seamless pathways to university graduation.

8

A STRUCTURED FOUR-YEAR UNDERGRADUATE PROGRAM

This chapter is designed to encourage universities to take a new look at the full undergraduate experience, assuming an influx of transfer students at the junior year, while also striving for coherence for both homegrown students and transfer students. (Thanks to GSU professor Maristela Zell for the term *homegrown* for students who begin as freshmen at the university in contrast to those who transfer. She rightly objected to the commonly used phrase *native students* to refer to this group.)

Many universities are working for coherence in general education. Northern Illinois University, Connecticut College, Appalachian State University, and others are committed to *integrated learning*, "which develops the ability to think broadly and connect ideas across disciplines" (Berrett, 2016). William M. Sullivan (2016) describes the consortium of 25 private institutions that make up The New American Colleges and Universities (NAC&U), which is devoted to "the power of integrated learning," as his book title denotes. Sullivan writes,

> The articulation of clear learning goals, effective modeling of what is to be learned, active practice of these things, and feedback on performance turn out to be the basis for developing expertise in all fields. These are the heart of effective education. (p. 4)

AAC&U offers summer institutes and workshops to assist universities in developing structured 4-year programs.

Alma Clayton-Pedersen and Ashley Finley (2010) describe the underlying principles of an intentionally integrated general education program. Connectivity is the key. Faculty members meet students where they are and guide them to "more sophisticated levels of learning" (pp. 2–3). Students understand the relevance of their studies to meeting career and life goals. Students widen their perspectives by learning from each other and from the different experiences that have shaped their classmates' lives (see box 8.1).

Integrated learning was always important to GSU—in principle—but the upper-division identity promoted silos. When every student matriculates within a major, departments tend to become isolated from each other. A positive result of becoming a comprehensive university was the opportunity to take integrated learning to new levels of implementation.

On December 6, 2011, IBHE approved GSU's proposal to move from upper-division status to become a full-service university, offering four undergraduate years. The memo I sent the next day to the campus community referenced two game-changing announcements. During the same week that we gained permission to plan a four-year baccalaureate experience, we received word from the Kresge Foundation of its support for expanding the DDP. We were on track to design a model undergraduate program as well as state-of-the-art transfer pathways from community colleges to the bachelor's degree and beyond—both/and, not either/or.

This groundbreaking dual focus on creating new options for degree completion was endorsed by local community college presidents. As was the case with the University/College Center at ASU West, the deep cooperation inherent in the DDP built trust with the community colleges, demonstrating that we were not playing a zero-sum game. In fact, our recruiting of freshmen for our own four-year program actually gave us opportunities to promote the DDP. When GSU was upper-division, high school guidance counselors had no interest in talking with our recruiters. Now GSU could promote two different pathways, one through the community colleges and another entirely on the GSU campus. The recruitment would be emphatically student centered, presenting the pluses and minuses of each choice. The centerfold of our first undergraduate view book highlights both the four-year and the 2+2 pathways. We cheerfully competed with ourselves by pointing out that the DDP sequence was less expensive than GSU's four-year program.

BOX 8.1.
Characteristics of an Integrated Undergraduate Program

Courses, programs, curriculum, and co-curriculum are made intentional when learning

- is structured appropriately, and students see the connections between their learning within various courses and across both programs and the overall curriculum, such as general education, the major, and other degree requirements;
- follows a progression that begins with learners['] existing knowledge base and moves them to increasingly more sophisticated levels of learning, it better ensures that students can scaffold the knowledge needed to comprehend more advanced concepts;
- aligns to achieve program objectives and programs align to meet overall curriculum objectives, learners can begin to make sense of what often seems like discrete bits of knowledge with no connections between them;
- is viewed by students as relevant to their lives—vis-à-vis the contemporary or enduring nature of the topic or a personal connection with the topic—it is more likely that they will recognize and value the lessons to be learned;
- expands to include learning activities in the community; the experience needs to be inclusive and respectful of the needs of the community and the community needs to be fully aware of and help facilitate having the activities achieve the expected learning outcomes[;]
- students' life experiences are understood and used to foster deeper student engagement in their learning;
- campus officials model respectful engagement with the communities with which students may interact; and
- differences between the students and those with whom they interact are used to enlarge students' understanding of people from different cultures and backgrounds—help students respectfully use these differences as learning resources.

Note. Extracted from Brownell and Swanners's (2010) *Five High-Impact Practices: Research on Learning Outcomes, Completion, and Quality,* pp. 2–3. Copyright 2010 by the Association of American Colleges & Universities. Reprinted with permission.

From December 2011 until the first freshmen matriculated in August 2014, we had the remarkable opportunity to design a structured four-year sequence from the ground up. Faculty and administration understood this good luck, and we committed ourselves to developing a state-of-the-art undergraduate experience for GSU students. We also had in mind that our work could be useful to other universities contemplating reform. We wanted to develop scalable approaches.

CCA, with its emphasis on guided pathways, core curriculum, constrained choices in the first year, and meta-majors, was highly influential in our thinking. Liberal Education and America's Promise (LEAP), articulated by AAC&U, provided a major guidepost. These organizations, although they do not agree on all points, have both been game-changers in undergraduate education at innumerable institutions.

Based on faculty research and creativity, GSU developed the following model four-year sequence. It is important to note that "general education" is infused throughout the four-year curriculum, not isolated in the first two years:

First Year (Freshman)

Homegrown students follow a core curriculum based on courses in the IAI, certified for transfer to any Illinois public institution. Students are in learning communities (cohorts), taking at least three classes with the same group of students. Freshman composition is capped at 18 students; all other freshman classes are limited to 30. Only full-time faculty members teach freshmen. Freshmen do not select majors but instead indicate meta-majors—general areas of interest—mainly so the students can be placed appropriately in either precalculus or statistics. Each student learning community is strategically surrounded by a success team made up of a math tutor, writing consultant, library liaison, financial aid adviser, digital learning specialist, counselor, career services professional, and cohort adviser. In addition, staff from the CJY assist students in identifying their mission—what they want to achieve in life—before exploring majors. The CJY and Career Services also help first-year students to identify prospects for internships and relevant on-campus employment. These services are also made available to DDP students at our 17 partner community colleges. For homegrown students, the first-year seminar in interdisciplinary humanities is specifically designed to develop understanding of the larger intellectual purposes of university life, with the selection of a major as an important component. Freshman core courses are infused with the following across-the-curriculum features: writing, citizenship, and living in the midst of art.

Second Year (Sophomore)

Learning communities stay together for the first-semester sophomore year, as homegrown students complete core curriculum requirements. Students avoid sophomore slump by trying out prerequisite courses for potential majors, investigating internships and less obvious career possibilities. The university places particular emphasis on the opportunity to major in something that may not sound like a job. Potential English majors, for example, discover that they know a great deal about writing for various audiences to achieve a multiplicity of purposes and that strong writing skills are imperative prerequisites for numerous jobs in business, government, and nonprofits. Liberal education, as it relates to career preparation, is an important motif. Students are thereby prepared to select a major in the second semester of the sophomore year. For DDP students, GSU staff join community college counselors to assist students in deciding on a major.

Third Year (Junior)

Homegrown, DDP, and regular transfer students come together in the junior year to form a new community within the major. To facilitate that process, students in each major take a cornerstone course. This course does not so much introduce the field of study—that is accomplished in sophomore prerequisite courses. Instead, GSU faculty members have designed the junior seminar/cornerstone to interrogate the major. Students form communities by asking questions together rather than by sitting passively as subject matter is introduced. About half of the cornerstone courses explore discipline-based research questions, and the other half pose ethical questions. In addition to integrating homegrown and transfer students, the cornerstone/junior seminar achieves the following two goals:

1. Transition: connecting the broad intellectual concepts from the general education course work of the first two years to the focused study of a particular discipline
2. Conceptual development: exploration of significant ideas and reflection on the nature of inquiry in the field

During both the junior and senior years most students participate in internships to apply learning concepts to real-world opportunities.

Fourth Year (Senior)

Students complete work in the major leading to a concluding capstone course, connecting the major to larger perspectives. The capstone is research based and interdisciplinary. Students reflect on internships engaged in during the junior and/or senior year. Those students who prefer to remain employed in existing jobs have opportunities to think about their work in new ways. For example, how does the study of sociology inform the understanding of customer behavior in fast-food settings? What marketing and service ideas might emerge from this analysis? To continue the architectural metaphor, the capstone places the roof on the major structure that began with the cornerstone.

Throughout the four years, for homegrown and DDP students, instruction is based on the strength model, discovering and building on what students already know to lead them to new knowledge and achievements. The co-curriculum is integrated with the curriculum, expanding upon students' leadership strengths and inculcating informed citizenship.

The overall design is built to encourage graduation in 4 years. CCA's 15 to Finish is a mantra. For students to complete a bachelor's degree (usually 120 credits), they must take 15 credits each semester. Stretching out undergraduate study beyond 4 years costs more, erodes academic coherence, and isolates students from their initial learning communities. We should consider the tried-and-true reasons for students to begin their intellectual journey as a unit and to walk together at commencement as the Class of 2021, 2022, and so forth. This social capital comes with the territory at elite universities. Although at regional public institutions it will always be important to offer flexibility to returning adults, students entering higher education directly from high school should partake in the incentives of graduating in 4 years and experience the lifelong social connections of being a member of a designated graduating class. Not every student who completes the 4-year structured undergraduate program will actually finish in 4 years. It's essential to provide opportunities for those especially challenged in the first two years to redeem early missteps through summer course work or even an extra semester, while still maintaining affiliation with their class.

Symbols are important. Starting in August 2014, GSU transformed its opening convocation from an occasion focused on a presidential address to faculty and staff on "The State of the University" to a student-oriented event, during which we welcome new students and celebrate the return of the rest. The procession symbolizes our values. The DDP juniors, now full-fledged GSU students, march in first and form an honor guard for the procession of GSU classes, with star students carrying the gonfalons indicating the graduation year. The relatively brief agenda includes the presentation of awards to excellent faculty members, advisers, and staff members. This spotlight on the highest achievements in teaching and learning is designed to build community within a framework of superb performance.

The march of the classes underlines GSU's commitment to a structured four-year program for homegrown and DDP students. We are not impressed by the suggestion of some policymakers that the baccalaureate degree should be trimmed to a three-year sequence. Nationally it is true that increasing numbers of students enter their first year with advanced placement and/or dual enrollment credit for college courses taken through local community colleges while students are still in high school. At GSU we believe that the vast majority of students need a structured four-year program to accomplish the substantial intellectual and social changes that give meaning to a baccalaureate degree.

Lobbyists for advanced placement (AP) have been traveling from state to state trying to convince legislators to pass laws requiring public universities to accept scores as low as three on AP tests as substitutes for important foundation-level courses. The AP proponents argue that families save money if students are required to take fewer university courses. Illinois has so far been able to fend off the direct-substitution mandate, but we are compelled to count AP courses at four or above for elective credit. We also are given little choice about accepting dual enrollment credits, even though they vary greatly in value. I suggest that proponents of the three-year baccalaureate take a close look at the Lumina Foundation's DQP (2014)—a document that guides GSU's curriculum planning. Would a normative three-year baccalaureate achieve the standards in that profile?

In some cases, especially for honors students, the accumulation of credits before university matriculation can make some sense. Students in GSU's expanding honors program who enter with AP and/or dual enrollment credit are placed in advanced and accelerated sections of foundational courses. These extra credits allow for full participation in the honors program service-learning requirements, open up opportunities for study abroad, and create room for elective courses beyond the traditional bounds of the major. Some honors students might even decide to graduate in three years, rather than four. But the promotion of a three-year bachelor's degree for all makes the mistake of treating higher education as a commodity rather than as a transformation. It has to be meaningful when we say at each year's commencement, "Welcome into the company of educated women and men."

How did GSU develop this structured undergraduate program—one that is worthy of this commencement welcome to new graduates?

In January 2012, the administration worked with the faculty senate to form and charge the general education task force, with responsibilities to report to the faculty senate. It was essential that the faculty senate be front and center in this major curricular transformation. Selecting the chair of the task force was a make-or-break decision. We were able to accomplish so much because the chair was a great listener, a diplomat, but, most important, a researcher. It might seem odd that a professor of physical therapy should prove to be the ideal person to lead the development of a general education program.

But GSU was most fortunate that Ann Vendrely understood the significance of general education for every academic discipline, including her own. Moreover, Vendreley knew the power of research in her own field and by extension in every university endeavor. She led the task force in a systematic investigation of theories and practices in general education. As a result, members of the task force developed recommendations that were informed by scholarship and data. Their work proved the principle that has been axiomatic in my career: Curricular change depends on scholarly exchange.

What resulted was a coherent design, not just for the first year, but for the four-year undergraduate experience. GSU faculty members were prepared to implement CCA and LEAP principles because of inclusive scholarly preparation. Teams of faculty members attended AAC&U institutes, workshops, seminars, and meetings, returning with a commitment to educate their colleagues. Carol Geary Schneider, then president of AAC&U, was our inaugural symposium leader in the spring of 2012, inspiring the campus as a whole to move forward on the topic of innovation and creativity in general education.

GSU's continuing program of symposia has done a great deal to transform the university. Since the spring of 2012, each semester we have invited the entire campus—faculty members, staff, and student leaders—to participate in an interactive symposium, starting in the morning and extending until after lunch. We enforce table assignments so that faculty, staff, and students have opportunities to discuss issues across silos. In the fall of 2012, John Gardner and Betsy Barefoot from the Institute for Excellence in Undergraduate Education led a symposium titled Promoting Engagement: First-Year Experience.

Subsequently, symposium leaders have led participatory experiences on teaching innovative thinking; WAC; ePortfolios; strategic planning; citizenship across the campus; and diversity, inclusion, and equity. These well-attended symposia have become integral parts of the university calendar. One indication of success is that participants no longer try to change their seating assignments but instead welcome the opportunity to interact with campus employees whom they do not already know.

Another important administrative decision was to organize and empower a lower-division steering committee. This cross-functional and cross-divisional group brings together personnel in academics, student affairs, admissions, housing, and marketing. The steering committee makes sure that what we advertise to students is what we are actually doing, that we are recruiting the students who would be best served by our approaches, and that we think holistically about the student experience.

Through GSU's study, strategic planning, and implementation of a structured four-year program, we learned—and continue to learn—a great deal. The following principles may be useful to other universities interested in fundamental institutional change.

General Education Must Be Pervasive

A strong, coherent first-year experience is necessary but not sufficient. Foundational knowledge, practical skills, social responsibility, and integrated learning must pervade the curriculum and co-curriculum. The infusion of writing, critical thinking, citizenship, and appreciation for art must be an overriding strategy, with intentional adoption by faculty across the curriculum. While still maintaining focus on specialties, faculty members must also be generalists, breaking down silos and helping students to see connections across the curriculum.

Teaching From a Strength Model Will Benefit All Students

Helping students to become conscious of what they already know—especially those things learned and enjoyed in nonscholastic settings—is the key to moving students forward into unexplored intellectual territory. Discovering strengths cannot be patronizing or trivial. This hard work is the key to teaching at all levels. Aficionados of the classic HBO series *The Wire* may remember middle-school teacher (former police officer) "Prez" Pryzbylewski teaching math by building on students' instinctive street knowledge of probabilities in dice games to lead them to a conceptual understanding of significant mathematical concepts. That may be an extreme example, but it makes the point about identifying strengths, changing the context, meeting students where they are, and focusing on intellectual development.

Limiting Student Choice in the First Year Paradoxically Can Prepare for Better Decisions Later On

First-year students often feel overwhelmed by the enormous changes from high school to college. We have discovered from interviews and focus groups that some students have gained the impression from well-meaning informants that they will be on their own in college, with no one caring whether they succeed or fail. Undoubtedly these advisers were motivated by the desire to inculcate independence in prospective college students. But expectations of isolation differ from true independence. "No one telling you what to do" is an erroneous conceptualization of adulthood.

Distribution requirements reinforce the idea of students being left to their own devices to navigate through uncharted waters with innumerable, high-stakes choices before them. A core curriculum, in contrast, provides a structured experience made up of an essential and interrelated foundational curriculum. Within this core and surrounded by a success team of advisers, peer mentors, and counselors, freshmen are encouraged from the start to think about their mission before selecting a major and to make informed decisions about overall involvement in university life. Limiting choice in the first year can provide a framework for more intelligent decisions in subsequent years of study. Although I would argue that this premise holds true for most universities, some, like Brown University, successfully promote a more open philosophy leading to increased individual choice and risk-taking in the first two years, especially when that approach is made clear as a distinguishing characteristic of the institution. One size does not fit all.

Themes Linking Freshman/Sophomore Learning Communities (Cohorts) Are Vehicles for Collaboration, not Mini-Majors

GSU's current themes—civic engagement, global citizenship, and sustainability—are overlapping to the point of being interchangeable. Their function is purely and simply to encourage connections among the three courses studied in common by the learning community and to stimulate ideas for overlapping assignments and drafting papers across the curriculum.

Within the cohorts, every GSU freshman takes at least three classes per semester with the same group of students. That requirement addresses one of the most daunting fears of incoming students: Will I make friends? Students may imagine that they will make friends at parties, but those who have formed lifelong friendships in college know that strong relationships are more likely to be built on shared intellectual and cultural experiences. The GSU cohorts are set up to encourage peer interaction, intentionally establishing the circumstances that create permanent bonds.

Providing opportunities to learn from peers, even more so than learning from professors, is an essential function of the university. Highly selective and prestigious universities have long understood that point. It's time for regional public universities to create circumstances for students to learn more from each other. At institutions like GSU that bring together urban, suburban, and rural students from every possible background, we have a moral imperative to help students build trust, communicate, and understand differing perspectives. In this way, the university can be a free zone, transcending neighborhood barriers and creating new communities of intellectual sharing and transcendence (McCabe, 2016).

A First-Year Seminar Introduces Students to University Intellectual Life

Although most first-year courses are under the purview of the College of Arts and Sciences, faculty members from other GSU colleges (Education, Health and Human Services, Business) can compete to teach the three-credit seminar in interdisciplinary humanities. The competition to teach this course highlights the importance of teaching freshmen and of the infusion of the humanities into the curricula of all four colleges. Faculty members teaching the first-year seminars bring back to their colleges and departments a heightened commitment to interdisciplinarity that will help in breaking down barriers across the university.

A Center for the Junior Year Links Lower-Division and Upper-Division Course Work and Experiences

Universities must take a new look at the junior year—the time when homegrown and transfer students come together to form a new community in the major. At GSU, the CJY introduces freshmen and sophomores—prospective juniors—to internship opportunities and careers based on majors in the humanities and social sciences as well as in STEM and the professions. Sponsoring and developing research on career possibilities within different majors, the CJY prepares sophomores to select majors in the second semester.

The GSU center does not leave the connection between lower division and upper division to chance. Faculty assigned to the center work with the director of general education, Career Services, and appropriate faculty groups to highlight general education capacities throughout the four undergraduate years. It's not enough to affirm the value of liberal learning. Students need help in transferring critical thinking capacities exercised in English, history, and philosophy courses to pragmatic settings. "Show, don't tell" is the motto of the CJY.

Campus Residential Life is a Living/Learning Experience

Midnight conversations about the meaning of life may not happen on their own. In addition to the usual assignment of resident assistants (RAs), each year three full-time faculty members live in Prairie Place, our student residence. They are assigned to work with residential freshmen on navigating their first academic year. In addition, they collaborate with faculty colleagues on communal academic experiences well suited to a residence facility, such as watching and discussing political candidate debates. Freshman cohort themes—civic engagement, global citizenship, sustainability—carry over into the residence hall, involving upper-division and graduate students in communicating with each other on these themes. The intentional development of Prairie Place as a living-learning community is another instance of our commitment to creating circumstances where students learn from peers.

Student Affairs and Academic Affairs Must Cooperate on a Fully Integrated Approach

Administrative structures can help or hurt. At GSU, the vice president for student affairs reports to the provost, creating a structure of integration. That reporting arrangement is not essential if the president mandates and enforces real day-to-day cooperation of the vice presidents. Student affairs coordinates the academic success teams, which function to support students during the first and second years. Whereas undergraduate and graduate writing fellows are trained for classroom assignments by the faculty director of WAC, peer mentors, also assigned to freshman courses, are prepared by student affairs.

The infusion of civic engagement into the classroom is strengthened by student affairs, which administers the Center for Civic Engagement and Community Service. During the Smart Start period in the summer, student affairs offers special leadership training to direct admits, who are not required to participate in the developmental writing and math courses (although we hope that some might be motivated to participate voluntarily). This leadership training includes a service-learning experience. Student affairs is also strongly committed to integrating GSU's non-DDP returning adult students in civic engagement activities. Returning adults remain an important segment of GSU's population and an increasingly significant constituency for colleges and universities across the nation. Student affairs has developed family-friendly service opportunities and has made GSU's multigenerational student body a distinct advantage.

Connecting Students' Studies With Career Preparation Should Be a Four-Year Agenda

Career services, which reports to student affairs, works closely with academic programs to integrate career planning with the structured four-year curriculum.

First-generation college students, who are in the majority at GSU, are especially vulnerable to seeking narrow vocationalism. Family, neighbors, and the media urge a guaranteed return on tuition investment and persuade students to major only in those fields that sound like a job. Whereas majoring in accounting, for example, is a fine idea for those who are intellectually stimulated by the field and want to be accountants, most students are unaware that all majors—whether they sound like a job or not—can lead to lifetime gainful employment and, in many cases, opportunities for advancement and leadership. When career preparation is integrated into a four-year agenda, students, no matter what their major, will gain skills in communication and critical thinking. They will also acquire experience, year by year, in the challenging tasks of transferring capacities from the classroom to career settings and explaining their ability to make this transfer to potential employers.

Clearly, like Jeffrey Selingo (2016), I am calling for wholesale reform of the baccalaureate degree. Selingo writes the following in *The Chronicle of Higher Education*:

> Employers I interviewed in a variety of sectors understood the critical need for broad, liberal learning, even if they didn't always use the language of higher education to describe it. Indeed, they told me that what will define *success* [emphasis added] in the future is the ability of college graduates to tolerate ambiguity in their jobs. The best of liberal education provides that nimble intellect. The jagged pathways to a bachelor's degree that are the basis of the experiments to reimagine the undergraduate experience provide students even more opportunities to practice their navigation skills before they enter the work force.

At GSU, we have implemented a model reform curriculum, validating liberal learning by the infusion of critical thinking, communication, and citizenship across four years of study. We continue to observe and evaluate students' navigational skills, nimbleness, and tolerance for ambiguity. We believe that the structure provided in the curriculum and co-curriculum offers education for the twenty-first century.

When the Higher Learning Commission review team visited GSU on April 15 through 16, 2013, it noted that GSU was transforming the bachelor's degree, as did John Gardner, president of the Institute for Excellence in Undergraduate Education, who commented on our development of a "unique foundational experience" (personal communication, n.d.).

My colleagues and I hope that this book demonstrates transformations on the order of what GSU has done are both necessary and pragmatic for universities across the nation. Even in the most challenging fiscal environment, we have prevailed by putting students first.

9

PUTTING STUDENTS
FIRST IS THE BEST
BUSINESS PLAN

U niversities are educational institutions first and foremost, but universities are also complex business organizations. The educational mission can be fulfilled only with sound business practices, but that mission cannot be undermined by business considerations. The two identities must be carefully and strategically integrated. This chapter discusses successful business principles and practices that are scalable to other universities. The overriding concept is that students ought to be the primary beneficiaries of higher education funds and that the money should stay as close as possible to the students, rather than in support of bureaucracies at a far remove from the classroom.

Let me say at the outset that many factors affecting the fiscal health of public universities are not under the control of university leaders. We can write editorials, testify before state legislatures, appear on news programs, and do all we can to communicate the message that public higher education is a public good—creating a better society for all. However, we have no choice but to recognize a prevailing belief in the general public that higher education is a commodity—something bought by individuals for personal benefit alone. Even that personal benefit is called into question through ignorance and distortion of facts. Study after study demonstrates higher lifetime incomes for holders of bachelor's degrees (Carnevale, Rose, & Cheah, 2011; Pew Research Center, 2014). Yet we continue to field questions about the degree's value as a commodity, whereas the overall societal benefit is not recognized at all. We must continue our efforts to change the narrative and at the same time develop new business models. As my current hero Joe Maddon, manager of the Chicago Cubs, often says in interviews, "We must control the controllable."

Developing new markets and budget reallocation, for both public and private universities, are two key approaches to controlling what is in our power to control. For GSU, developing new markets meant transforming one of the last remaining upper-division universities into a full-service institution, while continuing high-quality service to returning adults and graduate students. For us, freshmen and sophomores constitute new markets. Most other universities, already offering four-year undergraduate programs, must expand services to returning adults and community college transfers. GSU eagerly calls on these universities to compete with us in addressing the educational needs of these underserved students.

From an educational perspective, *developing new markets* must be defined as expanding the university's mission and commitment to excellence to new groups of students currently underserved by the institution. In other words, the business plan is to increase the number of students served and to put them first. Additional students mean more tuition dollars and, for regional public institutions, less dependence on state appropriations. For tuition-dependent private universities, targeting student groups beyond the traditional-age high school graduates means reaching new demographics. Budget reallocations within universities must move expenditures to where the students are.

In GSU's case, we expanded our service to undergraduates by providing incentives through the DDP for community college transfers to attend full-time and then by adding a model program for new freshmen and sophomores. At the same time we had to maintain and increase service to our traditional population of returning adults. Although GSU charges the lowest tuition in the Chicago area, becoming a full-service university increased our revenues, netting $2.5 million in the first 2 years. These additional revenues were realized because we kept expenditures in check while providing the structured 4-year program described in chapter 8. A core curriculum in the first 2 years benefits students academically and socially. It also costs less than a menu of distribution requirements with uncertain staffing projections. Full-time attendance (15 to Finish) not only benefits students educationally but also amortizes the initial recruitment investment. Uncertainty and incoherence undermine educational value as well as cost money. Our initial decision to limit freshman enrollment to no more than 300 full-time students allowed for connectivity in a core curriculum and predictability in staffing and class size.

The immediate and unwavering commitment to assign only full-time faculty members to teach freshmen accomplishes the educational goals reviewed in previous chapters. This decision also places strict limits on the adjunct budget, especially in the College of Arts and Sciences. Full-time faculty members now carry full loads, not always the case before the introduction of lower division. Influenced by the hierarchical fallacy, some faculty members preferred teaching sparsely enrolled (fewer than 10 students) master's-level courses to the prospect of teaching the new freshman classes that would not be large but would have a guaranteed enrollment of up to 18 for freshman composition and up to 30 for other general education courses.

One of the most important educational and budget moves was the successful negotiation in 2013 with GSU's faculty union University Professionals of Illinois (UPI) that equalized the number of teaching credits for undergraduate and master's-level courses. Prior to 2013, master's courses, usually scheduled for once per week for two-and-a-half hours, carried four teaching credits, whereas better enrolled, more frequently meeting undergraduate courses carried only three teaching credits. It was crucial to reallocate teaching credits to accomplish the goals of quality instruction at a full-service university. The pre-2013 system actually provided incentives *not* to teach undergraduates. That had to change. Through negotiations, a majority of faculty union members saw the fairness of this adjustment. With the new faculty contract, undergraduate and graduate courses all earned three hours of teaching credit.

Starting in 2007–2008, the first year of my GSU presidency, we paved the way for the reallocation of resources actualized in later decisions and in the 2013 faculty contract. One of my first acts as president was to establish transparency in university budgeting. Working with the faculty senate, I appointed PBAC, including faculty senate appointees and presidential appointees representing faculty, staff, and student leadership. This 17-member committee, cochaired by the provost and the vice president for administration and finance, meets regularly to review the university budget and to make recommendations to the president. All major financial decisions are open to PBAC review—tuition setting, student fees, and the allocation of resources to academic and administrative units.

Simultaneous with the establishment of PBAC, GSU undertook the formulation of a five-year strategic plan, Strategy 2015. The goal was to marry strategic planning and budget planning, investing resources in the strategies that would move us forward. The best way to be sure that strategic plans do not merely sit on the shelf is to link them with budget allocations and expenditures. Increasing enrollment was the top strategy in the first strategic plan and remains so as we implement the second five-year plan, Vision 2020. Through strategic preparation and budget reallocation, GSU has achieved double-digit enrollment growth since 2007–2008.

Each May since 2008, PBAC has held hearings during which budget heads of academic and administrative units testify about how funds were spent in the previous year and how money might be invested in the coming year to fulfill goals in the strategic plan. These hearings are open to the entire campus community. Every unit, including the president's office, is under scrutiny. From fiscal year 2008 (FY08) to FY15, state appropriations decreased, so PBAC's task was to recommend reallocations from less productive units to more productive units. Our preparation for adding lower division involved redirecting funds from other units to the College of Arts and Sciences and to student affairs.

The only year that we did not hold PBAC hearings was FY16. That was the first year that the Illinois General Assembly and governor neglected to pass a state budget. In fact, public universities received nothing at all from the state until April 22, 2016, not even reimbursement for the Monetary Award Program (MAP) state scholarship grants to low-income students. Assuming that no state would long continue such neglect of its state universities, we at first treated the situation as a cash-flow problem. Surely, the state would pass a budget soon, and we would adjust accordingly to whatever the appropriation turned out to be. As a consequence, we instituted a hard freeze on everything—hiring, travel, and expenditures of any kind over $1,500.

GSU was in a position to survive the situation because since FY08 the PBAC process had yielded carry-forward funds that we could put in a rainy-day account. Our intention was to draw on these funds for deferred maintenance—something that Illinois does not cover. With no state appropriation, we were able to use the rainy-day funds to meet payroll, as we crossed our fingers that our roofs would hold and the water pipes would not break.

On April 22, 2016, the General Assembly and the governor agreed on "stop-gap" funding for FY16, reimbursing universities for the fall (but only for the fall) MAP scholarships and providing for most institutions, including GSU, only 30% of the FY15 appropriation. At this juncture, we realized that we would have to make some immediate cuts that would inevitably involve personnel. We activated the UPI contractually mandated Academic Program Elimination Review Committee (APERC), with the goal of immediate budget reduction. Both APERC and the provost developed a list of programs for elimination. In August 2016, the board of trustees approved the provost's recommendation to eliminate 13 concentrations and majors. The APERC's report overlapped to some extent with the provost's, but the recommendations were not identical. The provost's eliminations included programs that had been on an enrollment watch list for at least 5 years—low-hanging fruit. Because confidential personnel decisions were involved for the first time in 9 years we did not hold PBAC hearings. We determined, however, that we had to find a way even during these hard times to reestablish this vehicle of transparency.

The late April legislative stop-gap with little prospect for an FY17 budget, which in ordinary years would be passed for the next fiscal year by May 31, 2016, showed us that the problem went far beyond cash flow and low-hanging fruit. We realized that we had to plan for long-term, significant reallocation of resources and further transformation of the university. On June 30, 2016, the general assembly and the governor agreed on a second stop-gap: covering spring 2016 MAP state scholarships (but nothing yet for fall or spring of FY17) and 50% of the FY15 base for an FY17 appropriation, covering the first 6 months but with no commitment to any more for that year.

GSU immediately had to make a decision about the MAP scholarships already promised to low-income students by the Illinois Student Assistance Commission (ISAC). As in the previous year, students who applied in time for FY17 awards had been told that the state would provide up to about $4,800 per year for the lowest income students. In FY16, the state promised the funds but did not fully deliver them until the end of the fiscal year. Some Illinois universities at that point alerted students that the university would allow registration for the next academic year but might hold students accountable for MAP funds if the state did not come through. GSU decided that we had to promise that no matter what the state did or did not do in terms of FY17 appropriations for MAP, we would cover student liability. We would not ask the students at the end of the year to come up with the money pledged to them by the state.

Our willingness to protect students in this way is a clear example of the principle that putting students first is the best business plan. We know that most GSU students who were promised MAP funds are first-generation exclamation point. With good reason, they have little trust in institutions, including universities. We also know that the most significant reason students drop out is worry over finances. If we did not reassure students that we would not ask them to reimburse MAP dollars, even if the state did not pay, we would lose them. We also know from statistics compiled by the National Student Clearinghouse Research Center (2016b) that GSU's biggest competitor is nowhere. Not only would we lose these worried students, the state of Illinois would lose future affluent taxpayers, and the students themselves would lose their on-ramp to the middle class.

But given our precarious fiscal situation, how could GSU afford to cover the MAP liability? Actually, we could *not* afford *not to*. Designated amounts for both MAP and Pell Grants (federal grants for low-income students) are determined by the FAFSA application. It's true that not every Pell recipient has been promised a MAP grant, because ISAC cuts off eligibility for MAP earlier and earlier each year. But every MAP recipient has been awarded a Pell Grant—up to about $5,800 per year for the lowest income students. If students drop out, GSU loses the students' Pell Grants. With the state forcing GSU to be increasingly tuition dependent, that is something we could not afford. Clearly in this instance, putting students first is the best educational and business plan.

After June 30, 2016, when Illinois did not fund MAP for the upcoming year (FY17) and allocated only a 50% (of FY15) stop-gap for FY17, we realized that we were dealing with an unprecedented fiscal problem. We could no longer live from stop-gap to stop-gap. We had to take on the difficult task of initiating orderly, strategic, and permanent budget reductions. As the fall 2016 semester opened, we put everything on the table, not only academic programs but also all budget lines. Strict zero-based budgeting is not fully applicable to institutions of higher education because a large percentage of the budget is dedicated to salaries for ongoing faculty lines. GSU, however, opted to examine every academic unit in terms of mission, quality, and enrollment.

In previous budget reallocation measures we had worked hard to protect academics and student affairs by making deep cuts in administrative areas. In this year of modified zero-based budgeting, we examined each nonacademic unit for further efficiencies, with the full knowledge that we might have to strengthen some of these units, Information Technology Services (ITS), for example. We also took this opportunity to rewrite civil service job descriptions to encompass twenty-first-century functions. Staying within the mandated state guidelines, we eliminated job descriptions that had been written in the 1970s and substituted positions we actually needed. This activity motivated employees to update their skills, particularly in technology, to improve service to students. Although this process may not save money immediately, it creates greater efficiency. As Chicago Mayor Rahm Emanuel famously said, "A crisis is a terrible thing to waste."

For the academic programs, Deborah Bordelon, GSU provost, did research on reallocation processes and rubrics used successfully by other universities. She consulted the work of R.C. Dickeson (2010), the leading expert in the academic prioritization process, in *Prioritizing Academic Programs and Services: Reallocating Resources to Achieve Strategic Balance.* The basis for GSU's rubric was developed by Humboldt State University and used successfully by California State University, East Bay (Cheyne et al., 2009). Provost Bordelon, using concepts validated by Dickeson's research, modified the descriptors in the Humboldt State rubric to fit GSU's situation. The rubric provides a touchstone for what it means to make fiscal decisions that put students first. (See Appendix B: Academic Program Elimination Review Committee Worksheet for the rubric.)

Program elimination had to go deep enough to allow for the anticipated addition of important academic programs that accorded with our mission and with twenty-first-century student demand. At the same time that APERC was working, the Committee on the Academic Master Plan continued the exploration of new programs. As we planned for further independence from state appropriations, we realized that we might have to make even more profound cuts to programs designed in the last century in order to add new twenty-first-century programs. We would continue without compromise to protect our commitment to general education in critical thinking, communication, and citizenship, because this strong educational foundation is essential to every major, to twenty-first-century careers, and to success in life.

We created online versions of additional undergraduate and graduate degree programs to accommodate returning adults. We moved forward on programs that we had previously put on hold, such as health informatics. Our planning now had to take into account student interest in such new areas of study. Throughout this "put everything on the table" methodology, we challenged faculty and staff to make radical revisions to existing programs to make them more student centered and current. We made it clear that lowering standards would be exactly the wrong choice. Programs had to be excellent. We could no longer tolerate anything that was simply adequate. Modified zero-based budgeting meant that everything was under scrutiny for high quality, as well as for relevance.

Our attempts to make lemonade from the lemons handed us by the state did not and should not take Illinois off the hook. Having no state budget is unconscionable and unsustainable. The plight of the state universities came about because of several factors, some generic, others anomalous. The funding of many state functions was covered by laws and court orders, leaving the public universities and human service agencies alone in the cold. Anomalously, the budget stalemate was caused by irreconcilable differences between a Republican governor and a Democratic speaker of the house, with the public universities as collateral damage. Some politicians erroneously and insultingly pointed to administrative bloat at state universities. As William S. Bowen and Michael S. McPherson (2016) point out in *Lesson Plan: An Agenda for Change in American Higher Education*, on a national level, although it is always valid to look for ways to reduce costs without compromising quality, "administrative bloat [is] a distracting but ultimately unconvincing claim" (p. 107). Given years of underfunding, it is certainly a myth in Illinois and emphatically not the issue at GSU.

Most states determine appropriations to their public universities based on enrollment formulas, performance-based funding (PBF), or a combination of both. Illinois does not. Around 1996, the nine Illinois public universities were in effect assigned block grants. In the more than two decades since that time—no matter how individual universities have changed—those predetermined appropriations constituted the base, which was then cut over the years. Other states instituted reductions in appropriations after September 11, 2001, and Illinois did also. Most states, however, increased allocations from 2004 to 2008. Illinois did not. In fact, during that period, Illinois, under a governor who was hostile to higher education, made further cuts. The Great Recession of 2008 brought additional diminishment of funds to most state universities, including those in Illinois, with some compensatory federal allocations easing the pain for a few years. In 2002, Illinois public universities were ranked as the best in the nation (as cited in Bode, 2002). It is tragic that the state has not sufficiently invested in that distinction.

From FY11 to FY15, Illinois state university budgets were cut incrementally. FY15, at the time, looked like an austerity year. Now, all stop-gaps have been based on percentages of that budget. Because the state provides no separate budget for deferred maintenance, state universities have had to find ways to fund repairs from their operating budgets. In FY08, the first year of my presidency, the board of trustees authorized the university to borrow to make significant repairs that directly affected the students' safety and well-being. As a consequence, the GSU campus became safer, more serviceable, and more beautiful. (And let there be no mistake about it—first-generation college students deserve to study in a safe and beautiful environment. One reason for GSU's founding was to maintain the option of a tranquil academic environment for Chicago students.) Since 2016, the budget stalemate has made borrowing virtually impossible. In spring 2016, the analysts at Standard & Poor's told GSU that we were doing an excellent job of running the university and paying our bills, but stop-gaps meant nothing to them. They downgraded us two notches.

GSU faces particular challenges because of having the lowest base appropriation, even when appropriations exist. GSU is a very different university from what it was in 1996. Our enrollment is now higher than that of two other Illinois state universities whose base allocations are at least $12 million higher than ours. So, when Illinois state universities receive 30% of the FY15 base allocation, our dollar amount is dramatically lower than it should be. In 2011, Illinois approved PBF, and GSU has consistently ranked high on performance measures. The state university presidents initially lobbied for PBF to be based only on new money, because we feared destroying collegiality by taking from Peter to pay Paul, as the saying goes. Because no new money was forthcoming, the presidents before FY16 argued that the funds distributed should be no more than .05% of the overall appropriation. As a result, GSU has never received more than $80,000 in PBF. Now, PBF seems to many presidents to be a fair way of limiting cuts—if not providing additional funding

A word about the collegiality of Illinois state university presidents—it has really been remarkable. The presidents meet weekly by conference call and several times a year in person. We elect a convener who sets the agenda and keeps us on track. I served in that role for three years from 2011 to 2014. Without an elaborate and expensive bureaucracy, we have cooperated most effectively. During my time as convener, we tried to draw on work at Illinois university think tanks to address the state pension challenges that continue to cripple the state. We take collective stands and write letters with all our signatures to protest state neglect and to encourage understanding of higher education as a public good. Peer pressure keeps each of us in line so that we function cooperatively rather than competitively. We reject the characterization of educators surrounding the wagons and shooting in. This collegiality saves Illinois millions of dollars. It's an example of putting students first by avoiding expenditures to support an educational bureaucracy far removed from classrooms and campuses.

Even as we focus on new budget models, we must check our peripheral vision for opportunities emerging on the sidelines. GSU serves urban, suburban, and rural students. Have we done enough to reach out to rural students? We have planned strategically for increased numbers of international students, who enhance the global perspective of our place-bound Illinois students. At GSU, international students do not take seats away from Illinois students because even with our double-digit enrollment growth we still have capacity. By paying double the price of in-state tuition, international students bring in much-needed revenue. How will we compensate for the educational value and the revenue as national policies adversely affect international student enrollment? How does a young public university like GSU plan for diversified revenue sources? How do we make ourselves indispensable to the region and to the philanthropic community?

Putting students first is emphatically our best business plan. The larger community understood when we announced that we could no longer use student tuition money to support the Small Business Development Center, which had served the GSU region for more than 30 years. In fact, Chicago-based small business centers contacted us immediately about new arrangements that would not carry a price tag for GSU.

On July 6, 2017, the Illinois House followed the Illinois Senate with a bipartisan override of Governor Rauner's veto of a state budget for FY18. Illinois had gone 736 days without a budget. Voting for a budget meant voting for new revenue, namely state tax increases, so the action was a difficult one for every legislator who cast a yes vote. The veto override included funding of the student low-income MAP grants for FY17 and an increase in MAP grants for FY18. So GSU's commitment to put students first and to cover these student scholarships was validated. The FY18 appropriation cut by 10% the FY15 budget (not "the good old days" but the last time state universities had a budget). That across-the-board cut would have seemed horrific two years ago, but everything is relative. At least Illinois public universities now have a predictable budget, rather than stopgaps, and can make plans. Those plans, unfortunately, will have to take into account diminished support for public higher education, not only in Illinois but also the nation as a whole. Yet, I would argue that the Illinois fiscal situation makes the point that if GSU can overcome unprecedented obstacles to make significant educational changes, other universities can do it, too.

We have accomplished and are sustaining GSU's transformation in the most difficult fiscal environment imaginable. Vision and strategy have made everything possible.

We have also been helped by the following scalable principles.

- It's essential to link strategic planning with budget allocations.
- Budget planning must be transparent and participatory.
- As much as possible, money should be invested directly in students, with a minimum directed toward systems and bureaucracy.
- It's a great help for a public university to have its own governor-appointed board of trustees, with full governance powers, including the setting of tuition and fees. Local power encourages public universities to be creative and nimble, as well as responsible.
- Private universities should capitalize on the advantage of governance by independent boards of trustees, who are also charged with fund-raising, to work with the administration and faculty on mission-driven approaches to putting students first as the best business plan.
- Although twenty-first-century technology should be incorporated into academics and administration at twenty-first-century universities, technology is not a panacea for reducing costs.

Putting students first also means affirming that higher education is not a commodity but a transformation. Liberal learning is the key, as we discuss in the next chapter.

10

LIBERAL EDUCATION AND THE SEARCH FOR TRUTH IN A POST-TRUTH WORLD

L iberal education is not a luxury. Thinking critically, evaluating information, solving problems, and writing and speaking effectively are indispensable capacities of an educated citizen, whatever the income level or career choice. Furthermore, adaptability in the face of change—using these broadly transferrable skills in new and unexpected contexts—is essential to twenty-first-century life.

Ideally, liberal education would start in preschool and spiral through graduate school. Universities prepare teachers at all levels, and we should help them bring into every classroom the implications of the educational paradigm shift from accumulation of facts to creating and applying knowledge through multiple perspectives. For example, first graders should be encouraged to see stories from different points of view, and we have excellent material to help teachers do that. If at six years old children have read *The Three Little Pigs* from the wolf's perspective as well as from the pigs', they will be better prepared throughout their lives to search for truth through evaluation and synthesis (Scieszka & Smith, 1997). Leading academic change means seeing the big picture—from infancy to longevity—and then developing transformative strategies for higher education institutions.

Vision and strategy in higher education, as described in this book, will determine whether we can transform the future into a time we wish to inhabit. Conventional attitudes lead to a stratified society, in which family income determines opportunities for higher education and liberal learning. Many low-income students never have a chance to develop their potential. Even for those who make it to the university, their first courses—the ones that provide a foundation in liberal education—are too often taught by contingent faculty at the bottom of the academic career ladder. Prestigious institutions offering incremental change to students who have achieved the best grades and the highest standardized test scores in high school receive the most resources, both public and philanthropic. Public regional universities committed to providing enormous value-added changes receive the least resources, impeding their transformative mission.

This tacit inequity, I believe, is the root cause of the anger and resentment that many U.S. citizens feel about their lives and, in particular, about higher education. When doors are closed to them, most people decide that they would not enter even if invited. For those of us on the inside, leading academic change is imperative. University leaders must articulate a vision for creating community across class, income, race, and gender. Making higher education inclusive is not optional.

This book calls for a broad-based commitment to what Michael S. Roth (2015) calls "pragmatic liberal education" (p. xiii). Putting liberal education and practical education into conflict is a false dichotomy, but this oppositional thinking is as old as the republic. Thomas Jefferson in 1779 argued in "A Bill for the More General Diffusion of Knowledge" that education in history and in "the experience of other ages and countries" would make people better citizens (Berkes, 2009). In contrast, although Benjamin Franklin shared the goal of education for citizenship, he was a harsh critic of liberal education as practiced at Harvard College. As Roth writes, "In Franklin we see two ingredients in the critique of liberal education that have remained potent until our own time: that academics are out of touch and that they tend to serve elites" (p. 100). A self-educated lifelong learner, Franklin founded The Academy of Philadelphia, described in an anonymous pamphlet (1749) titled "Proposals Relating to the Education of Youth in Pennsylvania," leading to the establishment of the academy in 1751 (ushistory.org, n.d.). This institution prided itself on an eighteenth-century form of collaborative learning. Roth described it as "mutual instruction, learning from one's peers, inspired a sense that effort, not privileges and wealth, would determine one's lot" (p. 99). Although Franklin's academy rejected learning for learning's sake, it incorporated many features that we associate today with liberal education. History, writing, rhetoric, and arithmetic were required. Franklin emphasized what we would call civic engagement with a specific appeal for service to "Mankind, one's Country, Friends and Family" (cited in Roth, p. 100). In 1779, the academy became the University of the State of Pennsylvania and is now known as the University of Pennsylvania, my alma mater.

This eighteenth-century history lesson is meant to show that *liberal education* in the United States, whether defined with Jefferson's or Franklin's emphasis, has always been seen as essential to democracy. In the nineteenth century, the land-grant universities were founded with ostensibly practical purposes, but from the start they connected career advancement with big ideas and big questions.

In Willa Cather's (1918) *My Antonia* the narrator, Jim Burden, describes his experience going from his family farm—a rather well-to-do family farm—to the University of Nebraska. He says, "I shall always look back on that time of mental awakening as one of the happiest in my life" (p. 257). No doubt, he and his classmates studied research-based ways to improve farming, but professors also introduced them to what Jim Burden calls "the world of ideas" (p. 258). Those big ideas included concepts of citizenship in a democracy.

For much of the twentieth century, universities and colleges in the United States achieved an implicit balance between career preparation and liberal education. Dan Berrett (2015) argues that this balance was destroyed on a single day, February 28, 1967. Ronald Reagan, then governor of California, gave a speech in which he said, "We do believe that there are certain intellectual luxuries that perhaps we could do without." When a reporter asked what he meant by "intellectual luxuries," the governor responded that taxpayers should not be on the hook for "subsidizing intellectual curiosity." Although reporters mocked this response at first, by the time Reagan became president in 1980, disdain toward liberal education as frivolous had taken root in American culture. A decreasing number of students were selecting liberal arts degrees, and business had become the most popular major.

Choice of major alone, however, does not create a diminishment in liberal education. The Association to Advance Collegiate Schools of Business (AACSB), the gold standard for business schools, articulates three core values—ethical behavior, collegiate environment, and social responsibility—all of which are traits of a liberal education (The Association to Advance Collegiate Schools of Business, 2016). Yet, it is undeniable, whether the perception of college changed on a single day or not, the false dichotomy between liberal education and career preparation has never been more pervasive or more dangerous (Colby, Ehrlich, Sullivan, & Dolle, 2011).

In research studies sponsored by AAC&U (2013), employers consistently highlight critical thinking, writing, quantitative reasoning, and teamwork as the most desirable characteristics of employees. But "liberal education" continues to be a misleading phrase. Members of the general public, understandably, immediately associate the word *liberal* with politics and reject the word, especially if their own inclinations are conservative or moderate. For some, *liberal* suggests permissiveness, a liberal attitude toward human behavior. Berrett (2015) comments, "The word 'liberal,' the association [AAC&U] acknowledges, has become a term of opprobrium. Recent research in economics found that top students from low-income backgrounds reacted to the term 'liberal arts' with comments like 'I am not liberal' and 'I don't like learning useless things.'"

In communicating with the general public about the importance of liberal education, it's almost impossible to use the phrase itself without being misunderstood. Yet, from the founding of the republic— in Jefferson's "A Bill for the More General Diffusion of Knowledge" (Berkes, 2009), liberal education is described as the best defense against tyranny. Today, as we search for truth in a post-truth world, liberal education has never been more important. As Roth points out, liberal education is essential for a democratic society's best work as well as for its continued existence as a democracy. "Citizens able to see through political or bureaucratic double-talk are also workers who can defend their rights in the face of the rich and powerful. Education protects against mindless tyranny and haughty privilege" (Roth, 2015, p. x).

In the twenty-first century, bureaucratic double-talk has been amplified on the Internet and expanded into "alternative facts" and "fake news." It has never been more important to teach students how to navigate the digital world and how to make sound and fair judgments within the clamor of social media. The Internet has transformative power—way beyond the revolution that occurred with the invention of the printing press—but that power must be channeled for the betterment of society. We cannot permit the voices of chaos and hate to drown out ethical and responsible discourse. I think often of William Butler Yeats's dystopian prophecy in "The Second Coming" (1919): "The best lack all conviction, while the worst / Are full of passionate intensity" (lines 7–8). Universities have the responsibility to educate students to direct passionate intensity toward creating a better world.

In earlier chapters we discussed the importance of foundational, core courses to empower all students to evaluate information, to make connections that constitute knowledge, and to apply that knowledge wisely to new situations. I would argue further that universities should rethink programs in journalism and media and should also consider incorporating media across the curriculum. People still enmeshed in a strictly job-related approach might argue that jobs in journalism and media are vanishing with the disappearance of print copies of the morning newspaper from the porch steps. In actuality, responsible journalism has nothing to do with whether the news is presented in print or online. What cannot be lost is the protection to democracy provided by the Fourth Estate. Sometimes called the Fourth Power, independent, professionally responsible news media are essential to the survival of democratic institutions. The famous phrase "Journalism is the first, rough draft of history," commonly attributed to Philip Graham, implies that universities and the responsible news media are natural allies in the search for truth and the creation of the historical record. Almost always, among the first acts of tyrants, is an attack on the responsible news media—and on universities.

Universities should continue to prepare serious journalists, well versed in the ethical standards codified by the Society of Professional Journalists (SPJ): "Seek truth and report it; minimize harm; act independently; be accountable and transparent" (SPJ, n.d.). Furthermore, universities should ensure that students majoring in every discipline are prepared with tools for distinguishing ethical journalism from the proliferating distortions and lies on the Internet and cable TV. It would be beneficial, for example, for every student to read or watch the film *All the President's Men* to see for themselves the fact-checking and rechecking imposed on Woodward and

Bernstein by Ben Bradlee, the highly respected executive editor of the *Washington Post*. On the same topic of Watergate, I would advise viewing *Truth and Lies: Watergate*, the June 16, 2017, ABC *20/20* documentary (Sloan, 2017). Since the break-in at the Watergate occurred several decades ago, this event has morphed from journalism's first draft into history itself. But the careful, ethical reporting of that first draft was essential to the historical record—and to justice and democracy.

DePaul University has created an exemplary Center for Journalism Integrity and Excellence, staffed by Chicago's legendary political reporter Carol Marin and her long-time producer Don Moseley. The center creates a bridge between the university and professional journalism, inculcating "adherence to the highest principles of journalism including truth, accuracy, fairness and context" (DePaul University, n.d.). Inspired by the DePaul center, GSU now has on the drawing board a Center for Media Ethics, designed to prepare college and high school students to cover local news in the Chicago suburbs, such as zoning board meetings, township governance, election of community college trustees, and so forth. Our tagline, with a nod to former U.S. House Speaker Tip O'Neill, is "All news is local." The idea is to promote civic engagement in the immediate environment, while strengthening the connection between international and national occurrences to where people live and work. Blogs and web pages have appeal because of this local dimension. We hope that our center will inspire individual journalists to adhere to the ethical standards of the responsible mainstream media.

New approaches to media education fit well with this book's affirmation of an epistemological revolution—transforming the purpose of education from simply absorbing facts to assessing information, forming valid connections, and striving for wisdom. This revolution requires change in classroom practices, curriculum, and the preparation of teachers and scholars at every level. It also posits different approaches to learners—recognizing and building on strengths, rather than focusing on deficits, as we have discussed in detail in chapter 6. This book promotes a vision of a broadly and deeply educated population, rather than one divided by income and educational access.

Implementing this vision requires the integration of career preparation and liberal learning. I use the term *career preparation* rather than *vocational education* because I hope that we can return *vocation* to its original meaning—a calling, often in a spiritual context, to pursue an occupation to which one is particularly suited, one that allows the accomplishment of a mission. In that sense a vocation connects earning a livelihood with pursuing a passion and doing good in the world. If we accept this definition of *vocation*, we can understand that career preparation without liberal learning is static, temporal, and trivial. Liberal learning without specific and intentional relevancy to careers and life is elitist. Many authors, including William M. Sullivan (2016), have written eloquently on the subject of integrating life, work, and society.

We see many references to the value of liberal learning in surprising contexts leading to unanticipated careers. In 2016, the *Chicago Tribune* featured an article about the work of art historian Amy Herman with first responders. Through providing experiences to look intelligently at artworks, Herman teaches firefighters and police officers to improve the observational capacities necessary to do their jobs:

> "We act as if there is only one true way to see. Our brains can only see so much and can process even less," Herman said. "I'm trying to use art as the great equalizer to point this out to people, so that they are receptive to the fact that we see things differently, literally and figuratively. Everything from our inherited biology to our learned biases influences the way we take in the world. Not only do we, as individuals, observe, notice and gather information differently, we also perceive what we've gathered differently." (Rockett, 2016)

Expanding on William Sullivan's, Amy Herman's, and AAC&U's perspectives, this book argues that liberal learning should be fully integrated across the curriculum and across the campus. Living in the midst of art and preparation for informed citizenship are then central to education, not something idiosyncratic and peripheral.

H.G. Wells (1971) in *The Outline of History* issues a challenge to all of us aspiring to lead academic change: "Human history," he wrote, "becomes more and more a race between education and catastrophe." Winning that race requires vision and strategy, leading toward transformation. We can change outdated educational practices and shake up old hierarchies that stand in the way of reform. If we do that, we will unleash the power of an educated electorate to search for truth and to create an inclusive society worthy of our highest aspirations.

High-Impact Educational Practices

First-Year Seminars and Experiences

High quality first-year experiences emphasize critical inquiry, writing, information and media literacy, collaborative learning, and other skills that develop students' intellectual and practical competencies.

Common Intellectual Experiences

Congenial with the intent of a "core" curriculum, examples of contemporary efforts to bring a measure of intellectual coherence to the undergraduate experience include a set of required common courses or a vertically integrated general education program that may feature a learning community experience often organized around broad themes such as technology and society, or global interdependence enriched with out-of-class activities.

Learning Communities

The key goals for learning communities are to encourage integration of learning across courses and to involve students with "big questions" that matter beyond the classroom. Students take two or more linked courses as a group and work closely with one another and with their professors. Many learning communities explore a common topic and/or common readings through different disciplines.

Writing- and Inquiry-Intensive Courses

These courses emphasize writing at all levels and across the curriculum, including final-year projects. Students are encouraged to produce and revise various forms of writing for different audiences

Note. Adapted with permission from *High-Impact Educational Practices: What They Are, Who Has Access to Them, and Why They Matter.* Copyright 2008 by the Association of American Colleges & Universities.

133

and disciplines. The effectiveness of this repeated practice "across the curriculum" has led to parallel efforts in such areas as quantitative reasoning, information literacy, and so on.

Collaborative Assignments and Projects

A variety of approaches have been found to advance learning from others and collaborative problem-solving, ranging from study groups within a course, to team-based assignments and writing, to cooperative projects and research. Such experiences are especially effective in promoting self-understanding and appreciation of alternative views.

Undergraduate Research

The goal of undergraduate research is to expose and involve students early in the undergraduate program with systematic inquiry approaches that introduce contested questions, empirical observation, technologies, and the enthusiasm that comes from working to answer questions or create new formulations through literary or artistic endeavor.

Diversity/Study Away/Global Learning

Most institutions offer some type of course program or experiential activity such as study away to introduce and have students experience communities, cultures, and world views that differ from their own, whether in the United States or abroad, with the aim of increasing understanding and appreciation of human differences.

Service-Learning, Community-Based Learning

Field-based, applied learning with community partners is an instructional strategy to engage students directly with issues they are studying in order to analyze and seek solutions to concrete, real-world problems, which also is good preparation for citizenship, work, and life. Key to realizing these desired outcomes is structured reflection about how classroom learning informs community practice and vice-versa.

Internships and Field Experiences

Internships and other forms of field experiences such as student teaching are increasingly common. Such applied, experiential learning provides students with direct experience in a setting typically related to their current career interests during which time they benefit from the supervision and coaching of professionals. Credit-bearing activities usually require students to complete a faculty- or staff-approved project or paper.

Capstone Courses and Projects

Whether called "senior capstones" or some other name, these culminating experiences require students nearing the end of their studies to complete some sort of project that integrates and applies what they have learned. Capstones are offered in departmental programs and, increasingly, in general education as well.

ePortfolio

ePortfolio is a portable, expandable, updatable vehicle for accumulating and presenting evidence of authentic student accomplishment including the duration of specific proficiencies and dispositions at given points in time. Done well, ePortfolio is a powerful pedagogical approach that requires meaningful student reflection and deepens learning while making achievement visible to students themselves, to their peers and faculty, and to external audiences.

Academic Program Elimination Review Committee Worksheet

Scoring Rubric Academic Program Elimination Review Committee (APERC)

Each program option will receive a score based on the enrollment, graduation, market trends, and costs reports in addition to program reports submitted to APERC. Additional data will be made available to the committee as needed.

Program Name: _____

Concentration/Strand: _____

I. Mission and Vision (15%)

(4)	(3)	(2)	(1)
The program curricular and co-curricular features strongly support the mission and vision of Governors State University (GSU).	The program curricular and co-curricular features adequately support the mission and vision of Governors State University (GSU).	The program curricular and co-curricular features minimally support the mission and vision of Governors State University (GSU).	The program curricular and co-curricular features provide little to no support of the mission and vision of Governors State University (GSU).

Note: Adapted from Dickeson, R. C. (2010). *Prioritizing academic programs and services: Reallocating resources to achieve strategic balance* (Revised and updated), published by Jossey-Bass and Humboldt State University Academic Program Prioritization (2009).

II.   Internal and External Demand (25%)

(4)	(3)	(2)	(1)
Enrollment in the program is high relative to other GSU programs and meets the Illinois Board of Higher Education (IBHE) requirement of an average of **40** majors over the past 3 years for undergraduate (UG) programs and **10** or more majors for graduate (G) programs (master's and doctoral levels)	Enrollment in the program is moderate relative to other GSU programs and is slightly below the Illinois Board of Higher Education (IBHE) 3-year average enrollment numbers.	Enrollment in the program is low relative to other GSU programs and is below the Illinois Board of Higher Education (IBHE) 3-year average enrollment numbers.	Enrollment in the program is very low relative to other GSU programs and is significantly below the Illinois Board of Higher Education (IBHE) 3-year average enrollment numbers.
All courses offered in this program have enrollments of 15 or more students for UG and 10 or more students for G. (Cross-listed courses enrollments are counted individually by level.)	The majority of courses offered in this program have enrollments of 15 or more students for UG and 10 or more students for G. (Cross-listed course enrollments are counted individually by level.)	Some courses offered in this program have enrollments of 15 or more students for UG and 10 or more students for G. (Cross-listed course enrollments are counted individually by level.)	Few or none of the courses offered in this program have enrollments of 15 or more students for UG and 10 or more students for G. (Cross-listed course enrollments are counted individually by level.)

(4)	(3)	(2)	(1)
The program meets the IBHE requirements for the average number of graduates (9 or more degrees conferred over a 3-year average—UG; 5 degrees conferred over a 3-year average—master's; 2 degrees conferred over a 3-year average—doctoral)			The program does not meet the IBHE requirements for the average number of graduates.
The program coursework includes graduation requirements needed by a number of other units.	The program coursework includes graduation requirements needed by only a few other units.	The program coursework includes graduation requirements needed by a few other units, none of which could not also be offered through other units on campus.	The program coursework is not needed to support other academic programs or university graduation requirements.
The program attracts and retains a highly diverse student population relative to diversity at GSU.	The program attracts and retains a moderately diverse student population relative to diversity at GSU.	The program attracts and retains few diverse students relative to diversity at GSU.	The program does not attract and/or retain a sufficiently diverse student population relative to diversity at GSU.

(4)	(3)	(2)	(1)
Current trends (labor market and economic projections) and employer feedback indicate that external demand for graduates from this program will increase over time.	Current trends (labor market and economic projections) indicate that external demand for graduates from this program will remain constant over time.	Current trends (labor market and economic projections) indicate that external demands for graduates from this program will decrease over time.	Current trends (labor market and economic projections) indicate that remaining external demand for graduates from this program will shift to other academic areas.

III.   Program Quality (30%)

(4)	(3)	(2)	(1)
Students participate in a variety of discipline-related scholarship/creative activities and service and recognition for their achievements (e.g., academic competitions, peer-reviewed professional conferences/publications, academic awards/scholarships)	Students participate in some discipline-related scholarship/creative activities and service and recognition for their achievements.	Students have limited access to discipline-related scholarship/creative activities and service and recognition for their achievements.	There is little or no evidence that students participate in discipline-related scholarship/creative activities and service.

(4)	(3)	(2)	(1)
The program has established and implemented a set of learning outcomes and accountability measures and has used the process to make improvements in the program.	The program has established and implemented a set of learning outcomes and accountability measures and is using the process to analyze the program.	The program has established and implemented a set of learning outcomes and accountability measures and is beginning to use the process to analyze the program.	The program has not yet established or implemented a set of learning outcomes and accountability measures.
All program faculty regularly engage in professional and reflective activities to strengthen their effectiveness in the classroom (e.g., student evaluations, midterm evaluations, professional development workshops).	Most program faculty regularly engage in professional and reflective activities to strengthen their effectiveness in the classroom.	Some program faculty regularly engage in professional and reflective activities to strengthen their effectiveness in the classroom.	Very few program faculty regularly engage in professional and reflective activities to strengthen their effectiveness in the classroom.
All program faculty are regularly engaged in professional scholarship and creative activities.	Most program faculty are regularly engaged in professional scholarship and creative activities.	Some program faculty are regularly engaged in professional scholarship and creative activities.	Very few program faculty are regularly engaged in professional scholarship and creative activities.

IV. Revenues (20%)

(4)	(3)	(2)	(1)
The program is operating at a high level of efficiency as measured by the student-faculty ratio, program costs, and generated revenues.	The program is operating at a moderate level of efficiency as measured by the student-faculty ratio, program costs, and generated revenues.	The program needs to improve the level of efficiency as measured by the student-faculty ratio, program costs, and generated revenues.	The program is inefficient as measured by the student-faculty ratio, program costs, and generated revenues.
The program requires a low level of resources (specialized facilities, equipment, staff)	The program requires a moderate level of resources (specialized facilities, equipment, support staff).	The program requires a high level of resources (specialized facilities, equipment, support staff).	The program requires a significantly higher level of resources (specialized facilities, equipment, support staff).
The program generates significant additional resources (external grants and other revenues) that help offset program costs per major.	The program generates some additional resources (external grants and other revenues) that help offset program costs per major.	The program generates few additional resources (external grants and other revenues) that help offset program costs per major.	The program does not generate any additional resources (external grants and other revenues) that help offset program costs per major.

V.   Potential (10%)

(4)	(3)	(2)	(1)
The program has the ability to grow with no new resources.	The program has the ability to grow with some additional resources.	The program needs significant resources in order to grow.	The program shows no promise for growth.
Investment in the program will result in innovation (delivery mode, curriculum, interdisciplinary opportunities) and the advancement of the mission of the university.	Investment in the program will result in some innovation (delivery mode, curriculum, interdisciplinary opportunities) and support of the mission of the university.	Investment in the program will result in limited innovation (delivery mode, curriculum, interdisciplinary opportunities) and support of the mission of the university.	Investment in the program will not result in innovation (delivery mode, curriculum, interdisciplinary opportunities) and support of the mission of the university.

Scores:

Mission/Vision:	_____/4	15%	_____
Demand:	_____/4	25%	_____
Program Quality:	_____/4	30%	_____
Revenue:	_____/4	20%	_____
Potential:	_____/4	10%	_____
Total Score:	_____/4		

Program Name:_____Concentration/Strand:_____

Criteria	Average Committee Score	Comments
Mission/Vision		
Internal and External Demand		
Program Quality		
Revenues		
Potential		
Overall Total		
Summary Statement/ Rationale		

Additional Recommendations for Reorganization and Restructuring of Units/Programs:

ABOUT THE AUTHOR

Elaine P. Maimon has devoted her career to transformation in higher education. As the fifth president of Governors State University (GSU), she has led the university in creating seamless pathways to student success: a model 4-year, structured undergraduate program and a widely recognized partnership with 17 Chicagoland community colleges, earning GSU the 2015 ACE/Fidelity Investments Award for Institutional Transformation. Maimon came to GSU with considerable administrative and faculty experience, always maintaining her commitment as professor of English. She has served as chancellor, University of Alaska Anchorage; vice president, Arizona State University, where she led the West Campus; dean of experimental programs, Queens College (CUNY); associate dean of the college, Brown University; associate vice president, Arcadia University (Beaver College); and assistant professor of English, Haverford College. An expert in the teaching of writing and a founder of Writing Across the Curriculum, Maimon has published many books, including *A Writer's Resource* (6th edition; McGraw-Hill, 2016). Her numerous awards include the Donna Shavlik Award for Women's Leadership in Higher Education (American Council on Education, 2014) and the Chicagoland ATHENA Leadership Award (2014). Maimon earned her BA (magna cum laude; Phi Beta Kappa), MA, and PhD (with distinction) in English at the University of Pennsylvania.

REFERENCES

Association of American Colleges & Universities. (n.d.a). *Degree Qualifications Profile*. Retrieved from http://www.aacu.org/qc/dqp

Association of American Colleges & Universities. (n.d.b). *Events: Summer institute*. Retrieved from https://aacu.org/events/summer-institute

Association of American Colleges & Universities. (n.d.c). *Making excellence inclusive*. Retrieved from http://www.aacu.org/making-excellence-inclusive

Association of American Colleges & Universities. (2013, April 10). *Employers more interested in critical thinking and problem solving than college major*. Retrieved from http://ww.aacu.org/press/press-releases/employers-more-interested-critical-thinking-and-problem-solving-college-major

Astin, A. (2016). *Are you smart enough? How colleges' obsession with smartness shortchanges students*. Sterling, VA: Stylus.

Bailey, T. A., Jaggars, S. S., & Jenkins, D. (2015). *Redesigning America's community colleges: A clearer pathway to student success*. Cambridge, MA: Harvard University Press.

Barefoot, B., Gardner, J., Cutright, M., Morris, L., Schroeder, C., Schwartz, & Swing, R. (2005) *Achieving and sustaining institutional excellence for the first year of college*. San Francisco, CA: Jossey-Bass.

Bateson, M. (1994). *Peripheral visions: Learning along the way*. New York, NY: HarperCollins.

Berkes, A. (2009). *A bill for the more general diffusion of knowledge*. Retrieved from http://www.monticello.org/site/jefferson/bill-more-general-diffusion-knowledge

Berrett, D. (2015, January 26). The day the purpose of college changed. *The Chronicle of Higher Education*. Retrieved from http://www.chronicle.com/article/The-Day-the-Purpose-of-College/151359

Berrett, D. (2016, August 8). General education gets an "integrative learning" makeover. *The Chronicle of Higher Education*. Retrieved from http://www.chronicle.com/article/General-Education-Gets-an/2373 84?key=OsGQ0pazKRHhAqcWyKIO2pDdTlBU6uf3EbyYsNZW2 KR4M2tvcXZKbm5rUVZwcTBJWkltb1A4NVJ6VTBZUHQ2VD-V1M2RHZG50Ykl3

Bode, G. (2002, July 24). Illinois higher education ranks first in nation. *Daily Egyptian.* Retrieved from http://dailyegyptian.com/32602/archives/illinois-higher-education-ranks-first-in-nation/

Bowen, W., & McPherson, M. (2016). *Lesson plan: An agenda for change in American higher education.* Princeton, NJ: Princeton University Press.

Bowers, K., & Lopez, S. (2010, February). Capitalizing on personal strengths in college. *Journal of College & Character, 11*(1) 1–11.

Browning, R. (1855). "Andrea del Sarto." In *Men and Women.* (n.p.)

Brynjolfsson, E., & McAfee, A. (2012). *Race against the machine: How the digital revolution is accelerating innovation, driving productivity, and irreversibly transforming employment and the economy.* Lexington, MA: Digital Frontier Press.

Busteed, B. (2014, June 30). *It's the educonomy, stupid.* Speech presented to The Education Commission of the States, Washington D.C., broadcast on CNN. Available at https://www.c-span.org/video/standalone/?c4502496/brandon-busteed-speech

Carey, K. (2015). *The end of college: Creating the future of learning and the university of everywhere.* New York City, NY: Riverhead Books.

Carnevale, A., Rose, S., & Cheah, B. (2011). *The college payoff: Education, occupations, lifetime earnings.* Retrieved from http://cew.georgetown.edu/wp-content/uploads/2014/11/collegepayoff-complete.pdf

Cather, W. (1918). *My Antonia* (13th Printing, Sentry ed. C). Boston, MA: Houghton Mifflin Company.

Cheyne, B., Escker, E., Hankin, D., Hopper, C., MacConnie, S., Oliver, D., & Watson, B. (2009, February 27). *Academic program prioritization: Final report and recommendations.* Retrieved from https://www.csueastbay.edu/about/planning-for-distinction/files/docs/Humboldt%20final.2.27.09.pdf

Clayton-Pedersen, A., & Finley, A. (2010). Afterward. In J. Brownell & L. Swaner, *Five high-impact practices: Research on learning outcomes, completion, and quality* (pp. 2–3). Washington DC: Association of American Colleges and Universities.

Clifton, E., & Anderson, D. (2004). *StrengthsQuest.* Washington, DC: Gallup Press.

Colby, A., Ehrlich, T., Sullivan, W., & Dolle, J. (2011). *Rethinking undergraduate business education: Liberal learning for the profession.* San Francisco, CA: Jossey-Bass.

Complete College America. (n.d.). *Corequisite remediation: Spanning the completion divide.* Retrieved from http://www.completecollege.org/spanningthedivide/#home

Complete College America. (2011, September). *Time is the enemy.* Retrieved from http://www.completecollege.org/docs/Time_Is_the_Enemy.pdf

Complete College America. (2013, October). *The game changers: Are states implementing the best reforms to get more college graduates?* Retrieved from http://completecollege.org/pdfs/CCA%20Nat%20Report%20Oct18-FINAL-singles.pdf

Conn, P. (1982, Summer). Combining literature and composition: English 886. *ADE Bulletin, 72*, 4–6.

Conn, P. (2010, April 4). We need to acknowledge the realities of employment in the humanities. *The Chronicle of Higher Education.* Retrieved from http://www.chronicle.com/article/We-Need-to-Acknowledge-the/64885

Cullinane, J., & Treisman, P. (2010). *Improving developmental mathematics education in community colleges: A prospectus and early progress report on the Statway initiative.* Retrieved from http://www.utdanacenter.org/wp-content/uploads/Improving-Developmental-Mathematics-Education-in-CC.pdf

DePaul University. (n.d.). Center for Journalism Integrity and Excellence. Retrieved from http://communication.depaul.edu/initiatives/cjie/Pages/default.aspx

Dickens, C. (1854). *Hard times—for these times.* London, England: Bradbury & Evans.

Dickeson, R. (2010). *Prioritizing academic programs and services: Reallocating resources to achieve strategic balance* (revised and updated). San Francisco, CA: Jossey-Bass.

Doyle, W. (2006, May–June). Community college transfers and college graduation: Whose choices matter most? *Change: The Magazine of Higher Learning, 38*(3), 56–58.

Eddy, P. (2010). *Community college leadership: A multidimensional model for leading change.* Sterling, VA: Stylus.

Egerter, S., Braveman, P., Sadegh-Nobari, T., Grossman-Kahn, R., & Dekker, M. (2009, September). *Education matters for health.* Retrieved from http://www.commissiononhealth.org/PDF/c270deb3-ba42-4fbd-baeb-2cd65956f00e/Issue%20Brief%206%20Sept%2009%20-%20Education%20and%20Health.pdf

Emig, J. (1977). Writing as a mode of learning. *College Composition and Communication, 28*(2), 122–128.

Felten, P., Gardner, J., Schroeder, C., Lambert, L., & Barefoot, B. (2016). *The undergraduate experience: Focusing institutions on what matters most* .San Francisco, CA: Jossey-Bass.

Field, K. (2008, July 25). Cost, convenience drive veterans' college choices. *The Chronicle of Higher Education.* Retrieved from http://www.chronicle.com/article/Cost-Convenience-Drive/20381

Finley, A., & McNair, T. (2013). *Assessing underserved students' engagement in high-impact-practices*. Retrieved from http://leapconnections.aacu .org/system/fi les/assessinghipsmcnairfi nley_0.pdf

Forster, E. (1910). *Howards end*. London, England: Edward Arnold.

Gallup. (n.d.). *Higher education*. Retrieved from www.gallup.com/services/ 170939/higher-education.aspx

Gallup. (2014). *Great jobs, great lives. A study of more than 30,000 college graduates across the U.S.: The 2014 Gallup-Purdue index report*. Retrieved from http://www.luminafoundation.org/files/resources/ galluppurdueindex-report-2014.pdf

Gallup. (2015). *Great jobs, great lives. The relationship between student debt, experiences and perceptions of college worth: Gallup-Purdue index 2015 report*. Retrieved from http://www.gallup.com/services/185924/ gallup-purdue-index-2015-report.aspx

Gonzales, M. (2016, May 25). Cubs offense breaks out for 12–3 victory to snap 3-game losing streak. *Chicago Tribune*. Retrieved from http:// www.chicagotribune.com/sports.baseball/cubs/ct-cubs-offensive-out- burst-cardinals-spt-0525-20160524-story.html

Gould, E. (2012, March 9). High-scoring, low-income students no more likely to complete college than low-scoring, rich students [Web log post]. Retrieved from http://www.epi.org/blog/college-graduation-scores- income-levels/

Guttman Community College. (n.d.). *Mission, vision, goals and outcomes*. Retrieved from http://guttman.cuny.edu/about/mission-vision-goals- outcomes/

Hacker, A. (2012, July 28). Is algebra necessary? *New York Times*. Retrieved from http://www.nytimes.com/2012/07/29/opinion/sunday/is-algebra- necessary.html

Harper, S. (2012). *Black male student success in higher education: A report from the national black male college achievement study*. The Trustees of the University of Pennsylvania. Retrieved from http://www.gse.upenn .edu/equity/sites/gse.upenn.edu.equity/files/publications/bmss.pdf

Harper, S. (2014). (Re)setting the agenda for college men of color: Lessons learned from a 15-year movement to improve black male student success. In R. Williams (Ed.), *Men of color in higher education: New foundations for developing models for success* (pp. 116–142). Sterling, VA: Stylus.

Harper, S., & Kuykendall, J. (2012, March–April). Institutional efforts to improve black male student achievement: A standards-based approach. *Change: The Magazine of Higher Learning, 44*(2), 23–29.

Hawking, S. (2015, May). *The theory of everything*. Presented at the Zeit- geist 2015 Conference, London, England.

John N. Gardner Institute for Excellence in Undergraduate Education. (n.d.a). *Analytics in pedagogy and curriculum: Guidance for a strong understanding of effective practices for applying analytics.* Retrieved from http://www.jngi.org/apc

John N. Gardner Institute for Excellence in Undergraduate Education. (n.d.b). *Student success and retention retreats.* Retrieved from http://www.jngi.org/events-2/

Kaplan, D. (2013, July 1). Calculus and statistics. *Amstatnews.* Retrieved from http://magazine.amstat.org/blog/2013/07/01/calculus-and-statistics/

Kuh, G. D. (2008). *High-impact educational practices: What they are, who has access to them, and why they matter.* Washington, DC: Association of American Colleges & Universities.

Kuh, G., & O'Donnell, K. (2013). *Ensuring quality and taking high-impact practices to scale.* Washington, DC: Association of American Colleges & Universities.

Levy, F., & Murnane, R. (n.d.). *Dancing with robots: Human skills for computerized work.* Retrieved from http://content.thirdway.org/publications/714/Dancing-With-Robots.pdf

Logue, J. (2016, April 21). Pushing new math paths. *Inside Higher Ed.* Retrieved from http://www.insidehighered.com/news/2016/04/21/tpsemath-working-reform-math-education

Lumina Foundation. (2014, October). *The Degree Qualifications Profile.* Retrieved from http://www.luminafoundation.org/files/resources/dqp.pdf

Magolda, P. (2016). *The lives of campus custodians: Insights into corporatization and civic disengagement in the academy.* Sterling, VA: Stylus.

Maimon, E. (2007, November 2). Installation speech presented at Governors State University, University Park, IL. Retrieved from http://www.youtube.com/playlist?list=PLwLZ8gE4BUfTU4TIx29cxc9_Qger77nlM

Maimon, E., Belcher, G., Hearn, G., Nodine, B., & O'Connor, F. (1981). *Writing in the arts and sciences (with instructor's manual).* Cambridge, MA: Winthrop.

Maimon, E., Peritz, J., & Yancey, K. (2016). *A writer's resource* (5th ed.). New York, NY: McGraw-Hill Education.

Manyika, J., & Chui, M. (2013, March 12). MBAs can't afford to end their math education with calculus. *Business Insider.* Retrieved from http://www.businessinsider.com/why-statistics-is-worth-more-than-calc-2013-3

Martin, N., D'Arcy, P., Newton, B., & Parker, R. (1976). *Writing and learning across the curriculum.* Upper Montclair, NJ: Boynton/Cook.

McCabe, J. (2016). *Connecting in college: How friendship networks matter for academic and social success.* Chicago, IL: The University of Chicago Press.

Merisotis, J. (2016). *America needs talent: Attracting, educating & deploying the 21st century workforce.* New York, NY: RosettaBooks.

Mintz, S. (2017, May 7). 11 lessons from the history of higher ed. *Inside Higher.* Retrieved from https://www.insidehighered.com/blogs/higher-ed-gamma/11-lessons-history-higher-ed

Mitrano, T. (n.d.). Re: The citizenship we are not talking about [Online article]. Retrieved from http://www.insidehighered.com/advice/2016/06/21/every-doctoral-student-should-take-course-higher-education-essay

MLA Task Force on Doctoral Study in Modern Language and Literature. (2014). *Report of the MLA task force on doctoral study in modern language and literature.* Retrieved from http://www.mla.org/content/download/25437/1164354/taskforcedocstudy2014.pdf

Morris, G. (2017, July 18). Eliminating community college to university transfer barriers—embracing co-enrollment. *The EvoLLLution.* Retrieved from https://evolllution.com/attracting-students/accessibility/eliminating-community-college-to-university-transfer-barriers-embracing-co-enrollment/

Mount Holyoke College. (n.d.). *The lynk.* Retrieved from http://www.mtholyoke.edu/lynk

National Student Clearinghouse Research Center. (2016a, December). *Completing college: A national view of student attainment rates—fall 2010 cohort.* Retrieved from http://nscresearchcenter.org/wp-content/uploads/SignatureReport12.pdf

National Student Clearinghouse Research Center. (2016b). *Governors State University* [Data file]. Retrieved from www.nscresearchcenter.org

National Task Force on Civic Learning and Democratic Engagement. (2012). *A crucible moment: College learning and democracy's future.* Washington, DC: Association of American Colleges & Universities.

National Writing Project. (2017). *About NWP.* Retrieved from https://www.nwp.org/cs/public/print/doc/about.csp

Obama, M. (2014, December 4). Speech (untitled) presented at White House Summit: College Opportunity Day of Action, Washington, DC.

Peden, W., Reed, S., & Wolfe, K. (2017). *Rising to the LEAP challenge: Case studies of integrative pathways to student signature work.* Washington, DC: Association of American Colleges & Universities.

Pew Research Center. (2013, April 25). *Civic engagement in the digital age.* Retrieved from http://www.pewinternet.org/2013/04/25/civic-engagement-in-the-digital-age/

Pew Research Center. (2014, February 11). *The rising cost of not going to college.* Retrieved from http://www.pewsocialtrends.org/2014/02/11/the-rising-cost-of-not-going-to-college/

Piaget, J. (1981). *The psychology of intelligence.* Totowa, NJ: Littlefield Adams and Co.

Rhodes, T., & McConnell, K. (2017). On solid ground: A preliminary look at the quality of student learning in the United States. Retrieved from http://www.aacu.org/OnSolidGroundVALUE

Rockett, D. (2016, October 16). Art historian helps cops, others observe better. *Chicago Tribune.* Retrieved from http://digitaledition.chicagotribune.com/tribune/article_popover.aspx?guid=cade4d20-7891-4633-8c4c-8d570a590de3#sthash.XaSr3rgQ.BWLBu81v.dpuf

Rosenbaum, J., Deil-Amen, R., & Person, A. (2006). *After admission: From college access to college success.* New York, NY: Russell Sage Foundation.

Rosener, J. (1990). Ways women lead. *Harvard Business Review, 68*(6), 119–125.

Roth, M. (2015). *Beyond the university: Why liberal education matters.* New Haven, CT: Yale University Press.

Scieszka, J., & Smith, L. (1997). *The true story of the three little pigs.* New York, NY: Puffin Books.

Selingo, J. (2016, April 13). Rebuilding the bachelor's degree. *The Chronicle of Higher Education.* Retrieved from http://www.chronicle.com/article/Rebuilding-the-Bachelors/236087

Shakespeare, W. (1606). The Oxford Shakespeare. Retrieved from http://www.bartleby.com/70/index43.html

Shaughnessy, M. (1975, December). *Diving in.* Conference presentation at Modern Language Association, San Francisco, CA.

Shaughnessy, M. (1977). *Errors and expectations: A guide for the teacher of basic writing.* New York, NY: Oxford University Press.

Sloan, D. (Senior Executive Producer). (2017, June 16). Truth and lies: Watergate [Television series episode]. *20/20.* New York, NY: ABC Television.

Smith, A. (2016, June 23). College students placed in remedial algebra have better outcomes in college stats classes. *Inside Higher Ed.* Retrieved from http://www.insidehighered.com/news/2016/06/23/college-students-placed-remedial-algebra-have-better-outcomes-college-stats-classes

Smith, A. (2017, April 11). Building clear paths. *Inside Higher Ed.* Retrieved from https://www.insidehighered.com/news/2016/04/11/community-colleges-trying-increase-pathways-students?utm_source=Inside+Higher+Ed&utm_campaign=0be8b923a0-DNU20160411&utm_

medium=email&utm_term=0_1fcbc04421-0be8b923a0-198193777#
.Vwv3ds4md8s.mailto

Society of Professional Journalists (SPJ). (n.d.). *SPJ code of ethics*. Retrieved from http://www.spj.org/ethicscode.asp

Sullivan, W. (2016). *The power of integrated learning: Higher education for success in life, work, and society*. Sterling, VA: Stylus.

The Association to Advance Collegiate Schools of Business. (2016, January 31). *Eligibility procedures and accreditation standards for business accreditation*. Retrieved from http://www.aacsb.edu/-/media/aacsb/docs/accreditation/standards/businessstds_2013_update-3oct_final.ashx

The Leonard Bernstein Office. (2017). Candide Overview. Retrieved from https://leonardbernstein.com/works/view/10/candide

The University of Iowa. (n.d.). *IowaGrow®*. Retrieved from http://vp.studentlife.uiowa.edu/priorities/grow/

Thiele, D. (2016, June 21). The citizenship we are not talking about. *Inside Higher Ed*. Retrieved from http://www.insidehighered.com/advice/2016/06/21/every-doctoral-student-should-take-course-higher-education-essay

Ushistory.org. (n.d.). *The electric Ben Franklin, education*. Retrieved from http://www.ushistory.org/franklin/philadelphia/education.htm

Vassar College. (n.d.). *Exploring transfer*. Retrieved from http://eter.vassar.edu/

Wells, H. G. (1971). *The outline of history* (new rev. ed.). Garden City, NY: Doubleday.

Yeats, W. (1919). *The second coming*. Retrieved from http://www.poets.org/poetsorg/poem/second-coming

Zull, J. (2002). *The art of changing the brain*. Sterling, VA: Stylus.

Zull, J. (2011). *From brain to mind*. Sterling, VA: Stylus.

INDEX

Page numbers for definitions are in bold face.

assessment strategies that lead to high-quality seminars. *What Makes the First-Year Seminar High Impact?* offers abundant models for ensuring the delivery of a high-quality educational experience to entering students.

22883 Quicksilver Drive
Sterling, VA 20166-2102   Subscribe to our e-mail alerts: www.Styluspub.com

Also available from Stylus

Degrees That Matter
Moving Higher Education to a Learning Systems Paradigm

Natasha A. Jankowski and David W. Marshall

Concerned by ongoing debates about higher education that talk past one another, the authors of this book show how to move beyond these and other obstacles to improve the student learning experience and further successful college outcomes. Offering an alternative to the culture of compliance in assessment and accreditation, they propose a different approach which they call the Learning System Paradigm. Building on the shift in focus from teaching to learning, the new paradigm encourages faculty and staff to systematically seek out information on how well students are learning and how well various areas of the institution are supporting the student experience and to use that information to create more coherent and explicit learning experiences for students.

What Makes the First-Year Seminar High Impact?
Exploring Effective Educational Practices

Edited by Tracy L. Skipper

First-year seminars have been widely hailed as a high-impact educational practice, leading to improved academic performance, increased retention, and achievement of critical twenty-first-century learning outcomes. While the *first-year seminar* tends to be narrowly defined in the literature, national explorations of course structure and administration underscore the diversity of these curricular initiatives across and within individual campuses. What then are the common denominators among these highly variable courses that contribute to their educational effectiveness?

This collection of case studies—representing a wide variety of institutional and seminar types—addresses this question. Using Kuh and O'Donnell's eight conditions of effective educational initiatives as a framework, contributors describe the structure, pedagogy, and

(Continued on preceding page)